MYSTIC QUESTS

MYSTIC QUESTS

By the Editors of Time-Life Books

TIME-LIFE BOOKS, AMSTERDAM

CONTENTS

In Quest of a Vision

The thirst for a dream from above,'' said the Sioux medicine man John Lame Deer, ''without this you are nothing.'' His declaration merely recognizes an ancient verity: Since the earliest biblical prophet set off alone into the desert seeking a divine revelation, no quests in pursuit of mystical goals have more strongly gripped human hearts and minds than those in search of a vision of spiritual truth. Native Americans, who believe that spirits manifest themselves to mortals in dreams, have long sought to satisfy this inner hunger in a ritualized retreat called the vision quest. The object of the quest is to encounter a higher being through a potent dream or waking vision. The vision quest takes the form of a journey into the wilderness for days of solitary prayer and fasting. Among American Plains Indian peoples—including the Blackfoot, Crow, Comanche, Pawnee, Cheyenne, and Sioux—it is practiced both as a rite of puberty and as a means of obtaining spiritual guidance at any stage in life. Women as well as men may undertake vision quests. Although details vary among different tribes, the quest has typically involved each of the stages pictured on the following pages, which depict a young Sioux boy's initiation into manhood.

The Heat That Purifies

The prelude to a vision quest is the *inikagapi,* literally "taking a sweat," the purifying sweat bath that precedes all sacred Plains Indian ceremonies. The ritual traditionally has taken place in a lodge constructed of peeled willow saplings bent into a beehive-shaped frame and covered with buffalo hides or blankets. The structure is tiny, standing no higher than a man's ribs and large enough for no more than a dozen kneeling men. "But to those crouching inside," wrote one Sioux, "it represents the whole universe."

Participants enter the lodge naked, symbolically returning to the womb of the earth. A pipe is lit and passed around, joining all present as brothers. Then rocks heated on a fire outside the lodge are handed in one at a time on deer antlers or a forked stick and stacked in a shallow hole. The leader sprinkles cold water over the stones with a sprig of sage, and searing white steam fills the dark space.

The lodge shakes with songs and chants, including a prayerful plea on behalf of the young boy about to embark on his first vision quest: "*Wakan-Tanka,* Grandfather, behold us!" cries the leader. "This young man asks You to be merciful to him. . . . He will soon go to a high place, and there he will cry for Your aid. Be merciful to him."

Alone on the Hilltop

Still lightheaded and dizzy from the effects of the sweat bath, the dreamer begins his quest by "going upon the hill." Accompanied by the elder who is serving as his spiritual adviser, he goes to a sacred place—the dreaming spot, as it is sometimes called. Typically located on a high, remote promontory, the dreaming spot is a small section of land marked off either by flags or by a pit dug into the hillside. Often the site has been used by previous generations of the dreamer's own family. This is where he will spend the next four days and nights.

For young Indians, who from birth have remained in constant physical proximity to members of their families and tribes, the isolation can be devastating. The Sioux later called John Lame Deer was a twelve-year-old boy named Johnny Fire when he went on his first vision quest near the turn of the century. Until then, he had never been alone in his life. "And let me tell you, I was scared," he wrote nearly fifty years later in a lengthy, evocative description of the experience. "I was all alone on the hilltop. I sat there in the vision pit, my arms hugging my knees as I watched old Chest, the medicine man who had brought me there, disappear. . . . I was shivering and not only from the cold."

Help from the Past

As darkness, hunger, and loneliness envelop the quester, he becomes acutely sensitive to his surroundings, his intuitive feelings, and the associations evoked by various sacred objects around him—offerings left by his predecessors or items he has brought with him. On young Johnny Fire's vision quest, he carried an ancestral pipe and a gourd containing forty small pieces of skin that his grandmother had cut from her arm—a traditional flesh offering, or *cheh'pi wanunyanpi,* the purpose of which was to comfort him by reminding him of another's love. "Someone dear to me had undergone pain, given me something of herself, part of her body to help me pray and make me stronghearted. How could I be afraid with so many people—living and dead—helping me."

Sometimes ancestors, as here, will loom up before a quester as part of the sought-after vision. Johnny Fire's sense of his forebears' presence was more visceral than visual, at least initially. "Blackness was wrapped around me like a velvet cloth. It seemed to cut me off from the outside world, even from my own body. It made me listen to the voices within me. I thought of my forefathers who had crouched on this hill. . . . I could sense their presence right through the earth I was leaning against. I could feel them entering my body, feel them stirring in my mind and heart."

Overwhelmed by a Presence

The climax of the quest typically comes as a dramatic visitation from a manifestation of a higher power, sometimes called the Great Mystery Power or the Grandfather Spirit.

"Suddenly I felt an overwhelming presence," John Lame Deer remembered, half a century after his quest. "Down there with me in my cramped hole was a huge bird . . . flying around me as if he had the whole sky to himself. I could hear his cries, sometimes near, sometimes far, far away. I could feel feathers or a wing touching my back and head. . . . I trembled and my bones turned to ice. . . . All at once, I was way up there with the birds. I could look down, even on the stars, and the Moon was close to my left side. A voice said, 'You are sacrificing yourself here to become a medicine man. In time you will be one.' "

Then an image appeared. "I saw that this was my great-grandfather Tahca Ushte, Lame Deer, chief of the Minneconjou. I understood that my great-grandfather wished me to take his name. This made me glad beyond words.

"I don't know how long I had been up there, one minute or a lifetime. I felt a hand on my shoulder gently shaking me. It was Uncle Chest who had come for me. 'You have been up here four days, hokshila,' he told me. 'Time to come down.' "

Finding Guidance in the Dream

Back in his village, the candidate joins the men—who now accept him as an equal—to relate what he has experienced. The guiding elder then interprets the vision and tells the quester what to do to maintain personal spiritual continuity throughout the years ahead.

Often the ceremony also involves conferring symbols of the quest on the successful seeker. Here the young man receives a hide shield painted with a representation of the spirit bird that came to him in his vision. The bird now becomes his spiritual protector. Initiates sometimes receive a new name as well.

This final ceremony not only defines the weight and meaning of the whole vision quest for the seeker, it also gives the tribe the opportunity to share in the individual's experience. In many Plains bands, in fact, tradition said the vision assumed its power only when the quester acted it out for the tribe. This added the mystical power of the vision to the group's common spiritual strength.

But for young Johnny Fire, perhaps, the community's reward was no greater than his own sense of personal achievement when his Uncle Chest, who had served as his guide to the hidden meanings of his experience on the mountain, welcomed him back from his vision quest. "He told me that I was no longer a boy, that I was a man now. I was Lame Deer."

CHAPTER 1

Beyond the Horizon

Public officials have often needed rescuing from the effects of their private behavior, and one of the more unusual exercises in political damage control fell to Harry Hopkins, longtime adviser to President Franklin Delano Roosevelt. Hopkins rendered his services in the summer of 1940, not to smooth over anything his boss had said or done, but to salvage the reputation of Henry A. Wallace, FDR's two-term secretary of agriculture. Wallace had just been chosen to be the Democratic party's vice-presidential candidate in the upcoming election, and Republican strategists were licking their chops at the prospect of turning his personal foibles into political liabilities. According to Hopkins's network of spies, press reports were being prepared that would probe the candidate's ties to a little-known mystical cult and expose his highly unorthodox view that the Second Coming had transpired in a remote Asian kingdom called Shambhala.

Henry Wallace had, in some regards, been an effective cabinet officer. He was an accomplished plant geneticist and had made the most of a solid expertise in agricultural matters at a time when the federal government was heavily involved in helping American farmers. But he was also an eccentric man in many ways, particularly when it came to the very personal matter of his religious convictions. The problem was not a lack of interest on his part—if anything, just the opposite.

Wallace was, in the phrase of conservative newspaper columnist Westbrook Pegler, a sort of "spiritual window-shopper." He was born and raised a Presbyterian but had decided early on that his parents' religion was too stark and unemotional for his tastes. He dabbled with Roman Catholicism for a time, delighted by the elaborate rituals of that faith, but then shifted to Episcopalianism, taking on the role of an acolyte and donning cassock and surplice for service at the eight o'clock Mass. If matters had gone no further than this, Harry Hopkins would have had no problem. But Wallace's thirst for spiritual experience was never slaked for long.

Over the years, Wallace sampled a great many religious creeds, studying Buddhism, Zoroastrianism, Islam, and Christian Science, among others. He also investigated secret societies and Eastern cults, developing a fondness for the arcane symbols and practices favored by such groups. By the time he entered politics, Wallace had incorporated bits and pieces of these many forms of worship and magic into a highly idiosyncratic religious view. He would later describe his personal faith as a form of pantheism in which science, nature, and religion were all one and the same—this in an era when Middle America was not so tolerant of exotic spiritual ideas as it would later become.

Not long after Wallace assumed his post at the Department of Agriculture, he became acquainted with a strangely charismatic Russian émigré named Nikolay Konstantinovich Roerich. A painter by profession, Roerich looked more like a Chinese alchemist or perhaps a Buddhist monk. He was a small man with a bald head, a long white goatee, and a soothingly quiet voice.

The Russian had achieved his most lasting notoriety in 1913, when he designed sets and costumes for the premiere in Paris of Igor Stravinsky's controversial ballet *The Rite of Spring,* which had featured dancer Vaslav Nijinsky. By 1933, however, Roerich's artistic contributions were largely behind him, and he had given himself over to consuming interests in Russian politics and mystical experience. In pursuit of the latter, he had traveled extensively across Asia, making lengthy visits to China, Mongolia, Tibet, Sikkim, Kashmir, and Turkistan.

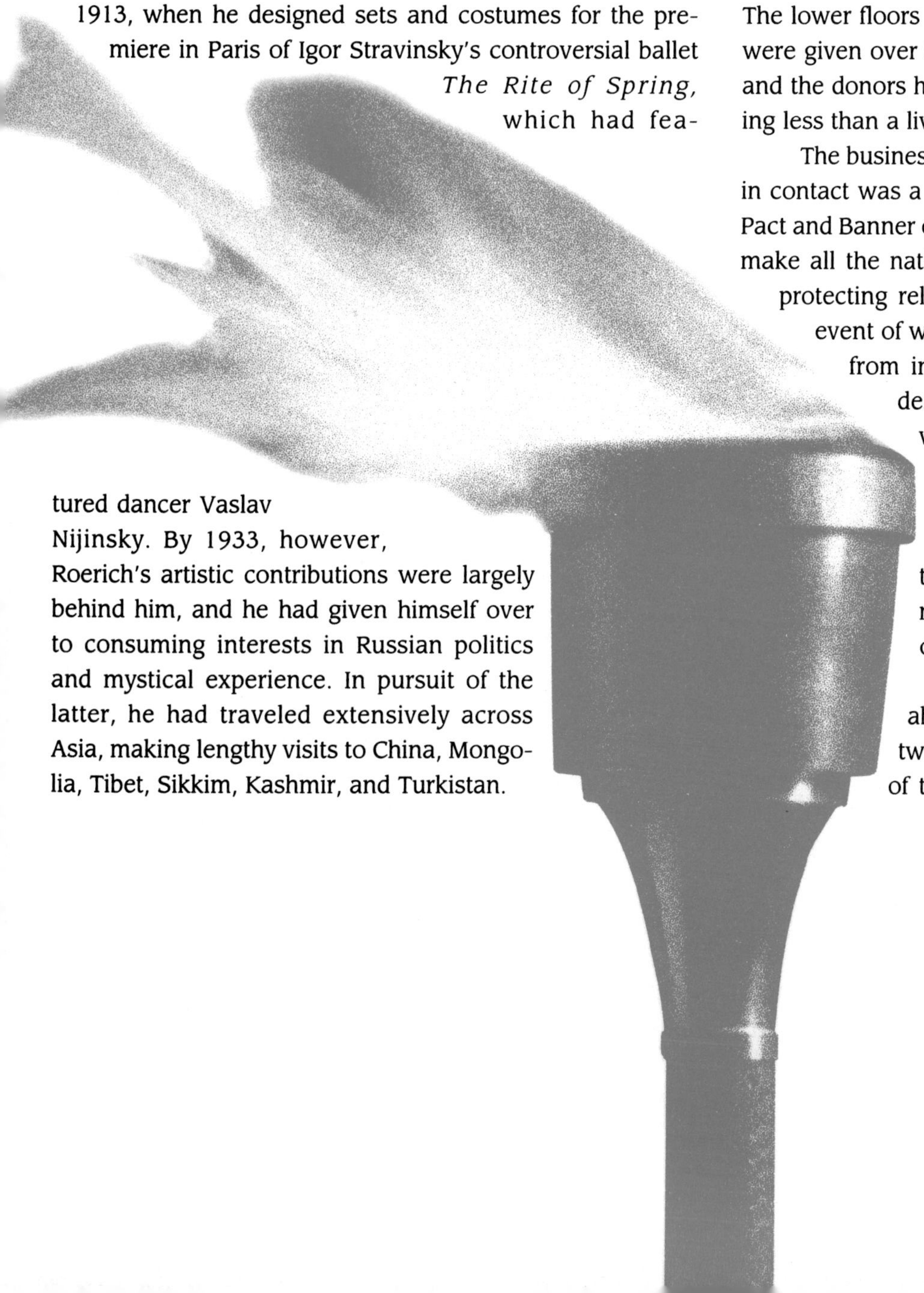

Somewhere along the line, Roerich became involved with the Theosophical Society, a mystical organization established in the nineteenth century by another, more illustrious, Russian émigré, Helena Petrovna Blavatsky. The Theosophists had made it their business to inculcate the West with the teachings of Eastern religions and various mystical philosophies. And in keeping with a pattern established by leaders of this group, Roerich set himself up as a guru to a small circle of admirers. Among his supporters in Europe were the Nobel Prize-winning Hindu poet Rabindranath Tagore and composer Nikolay Rimsky-Korsakov. But Roerich found a particularly warm embrace in the United States, where he attracted a circle of wealthy devotees.

By the time he crossed paths with Henry Wallace, he was ensconced in a twenty-nine-story apartment house built for his purposes on Riverside Drive in New York City. The lower floors of this nearly three-million-dollar building were given over to a vast collection of Roerich's paintings, and the donors had come to think of their teacher as nothing less than a living deity.

The business matter that brought Roerich and Wallace in contact was a pet project of the guru called the Roerich Pact and Banner of Peace. This was an ambitious scheme to make all the nations of earth signatories to a convention protecting religious sites and cultural treasures in the event of war. In concept, the pact was little different from international agreements forswearing the destruction of hospitals in battle. Wallace was so taken with Roerich's plan—and promoted it so energetically—that in 1935, delegates from twenty-one nations turned out to put their names to the agreement at a White House ceremony. Franklin Roosevelt himself presided over the gathering.

Not much is known with certainty about the relationship that developed between Wallace and Roerich in the aftermath of this successful venture. They met face to

Painter, guru, would-be statesman, and ardent seeker of Shambhala, Russian émigré Nikolay Roerich strikes a typically enigmatic pose in the photographic portrait at right. Under his utopian Roerich Pact, nations agreed that in time of war they would endeavor to preserve cultural and religious sites marked with the symbol shown below. The three spheres of the emblem, Roerich said, represented culture, spirit, and humanity.

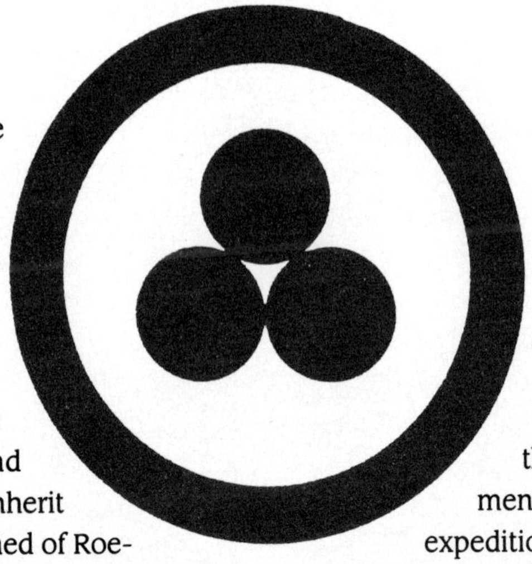

face only once, but it appears that the cabinet officer took it upon himself to master the Russian's teachings. In the process, he would certainly have pondered one of the guru's central obsessions—the quest for Shambhala. As depicted in Roerich's writings, Shambhala was a hidden place where holy men studied an enlightened way of life and waited for the time when they would inherit the earth. Wallace would also have learned of Roerich's belief that Christ had been reincarnated in India. It is not clear whether the connection between Shambhala and the biblically prophesied return of the Savior was suggested by Roerich or was the product of Wallace's own wishful thinking. But either way, the idea that Christ may be alive in Shambhala took root in the secretary's imagination.

Wallace corresponded with Roerich and his wife, Helena Ivanovna Shaposhnikov, on a regular basis, seeking their advice on a wide variety of matters. Letters produced in this correspondence—begun "Dear Guru" and signed "H. A. Wallace" or "HAW," some of them even typed on Department of Agriculture letterhead—would later be a source of controversy. They were at the root of Harry Hopkins's worries during the 1940 election. But that was still several years in the future, after Wallace and Roerich had gone their separate ways.

In the meantime, Wallace's fascination with his new teacher yielded two concrete results. The first was that the secretary persuaded his fellow cabinet officer, Secretary of the Treasury Henry Morgenthau, Jr., to make a change in the U.S. currency. An exotic-looking symbol of a pyramid with an all-seeing eye at its apex had long been part of the Great Seal of the United States. At Roerich's urging, Wallace convinced his colleague to make the symbol a fixture on the back of every one-dollar bill. Morgenthau later claimed that it was not until after the change had been made that he learned of the pyramid's "cabalistic significance for members of a small religious sect."

The other outgrowth of the Wallace-Roerich association was that the secretary put the guru on the government payroll, directing him to lead a scientific expedition to Outer Mongolia and Tibet. This unusual mission was given a staid-sounding official rationale: The party was to investigate the drought-resistant grasses of Asia in hopes of reviving the parched farmlands of the south central United States, which had come to be known as the Dust Bowl. To give substance to this story, Wallace staffed up the project with two serious-minded plant scientists. Along the halls of the Department of Agriculture in Washington, however, the true purpose of the mission was no great secret: Roerich would be making his journey to the East to search for Shambhala.

Roerich was accompanied on this tour of Asia by his

Franklin Roosevelt looks on benignly as the guru's patron, Secretary of Agriculture Henry A. Wallace, signs the Roerich Pact in 1935. Although less mystically inclined than Wallace, Roosevelt did correspond with Mrs. Roerich, who described him as a man of destiny.

son. The two men stayed always a step ahead of the frustrated plant experts from Washington, who were meant to be under their direction. If Roerich hoodwinked the Agriculture Department in this respect, however, he must have also bewildered Henry Wallace with his seeming lack of interest in Shambhala or the Second Coming. As nearly as can be determined, Roerich spent his time laying the groundwork for an armed incursion into eastern Russia, where he hoped to establish an independent state—a coup d'état that never materialized. Needless to say, the State Department was inconvenienced by his comings and goings in Asia.

The guru's government ties served him well and lasted for about two years, ending at the same time as his friendship with Wallace. No details are known about the falling out, but through a complicated chain of events the matter became the subject of an abortive lawsuit, and that had the effect of putting Wallace's letters into circulation. For years afterward, awkward rumors circulated about the secretary's peculiar friends and superstitions.

Harry Hopkins was able to get Wallace over the hump in the 1940 election by the straightforward expedients of intimidating appropriate newspaper publishers and brandishing threats about the damage he could do in return to the reputations of Republican candidates. But the letters caught up with Henry Wallace in the end. When they were finally published in 1948, Wallace denied all knowledge of the correspondence, implying that the letters were forgeries. Many people did not believe him, however, and few historians doubt that the letters were actually his. One scholar, Edwin Bernbaum, a specialist in Buddhist legends, made the observation that "if Roosevelt had died before the 1944 election instead of after it, a man deeply influenced by the Tibetan myth of Shambhala would have become President of the United States." As it was, Wallace's fascination with Shambhala destroyed his political career.

For his part, Nikolay Roerich was a complex man with enough of the con artist in him that it is not easy to say with certainty what the full range of his motives was in his dealings with Henry Wallace. On the surface, it would seem that he simply took advantage of his highly placed disciple to open doors for himself. By the time of his stint as a government consultant, however, Roerich had traveled for many years in Asia and had devoted a great deal of energy to the study of Eastern philosophy. He had written so passionately about Shambhala that it is difficult to assume that his whole purpose was limited to fulfilling his political goals. It seems much more likely that the search for a hidden kingdom of enlightened humanity was extraordinarily important to Roerich, as it was to Wallace.

History indicates that such mystical ideas as the fabulous kingdom of Shambhala can number among the most compelling goals in human experience. Be it a legendary place, like Shambhala or Camelot, or a storied object that may or may not ever have existed, or a special spiritual experience, difficult to attain and perhaps believed to confer an extraordinary power—an idea can become an obsession that dwarfs more common life objectives such as work, money, family, happiness, or fame. People who are smitten by the desire—or need—to achieve one of these mystical goals share a common sense of urgency that sometimes leads them to set aside all other concerns. They may abandon the comforts of their homes and risk their fortunes, careers, reputations, even their lives to pursue a notion that friends and onlookers often view as a downright crackpot fixation, or at best as a far-fetched and elusive chimera.

Some of these quests strike a resonant chord in the human imagination and become obsessions for literally thousands of people over the course of many centuries. One that has shown a sort of timeless appeal is the quest for physical immortality, which continues unabated today. In earlier times, the desire to cheat death led quasi-scientific investigators such as the alchemists of the fifteenth through seventeenth centuries to squirrel themselves away in laboratories—in some cases for their entire lifetimes—looking for the key to everlasting health. Once embarked on this all-consuming mission, most of them accomplished little more than the ruination of their health, but the dream was enough to carry them on. The same hope for unrivaled longevity lured many Spaniards to tramp for years through the unexplored wilds of America in hopes of drinking from the Fountain of Youth. The reward for most of them was instead an early death. Other quests that have repeatedly fired the ambitions of adventurers and zealots include the searches for Noah's Ark and for the Holy Grail.

In contrast to these widely recognized goals are others that are a little more idiosyncratic and, often, highly personal in their motivation. Among the latter are the efforts of religious fundamentalists to prove the literal truth of sacred texts by verifying the historical accuracy of their contents. Such endeavors have occasionally drawn the most determined of questers to undertake highly improbable measures, such as combing the Peruvian highlands for traces of King Solomon's mines, or scuba diving in the Dead Sea on the outside chance of turning up Sodom and Gomorrah.

As preserved in the religious teachings and folklore of Tibet, the obscure Asian kingdom that fascinated Nikolay Roerich and caused such problems for Henry Wallace is an extremely elusive place. To the Tibetans, Shambhala is a mystical land somewhere to the north, where a succession of powerful yet supremely patient kings await the preordained moment when they will sweep aside the armies of less enlightened monarchs and usher in a golden age of wisdom and peace. Until that time, the rulers of Shambhala are content to reign over an earthly paradise where they safeguard the most closely held secrets of Buddhism.

In the view of the Tibetans, it is not impossible to travel overland to the hidden kingdom, as Roerich attempted to do. But the journey is reputed to be extraordinarily arduous and filled with many perils—it is not regarded as a wise undertaking. Going to Shambhala involves crossing vast tracts of mountains and desert, and overcoming obstacles thrown in the way by the protective deities of the kingdom. All in all, the pilgrim is deemed more than likely to fail, and for that reason the Buddhists believe that a spiritual journey is the best course of action. Even this approach has its problems, however, for only those who have achieved a suitable karma can realistically hope to succeed. Shambhala, the Tibetans maintain, is the last stop on the path to nirvana.

References to the mystical kingdom began appearing in the writings of lamas, or Buddhist priests, around the eleventh century AD. As described in these old texts, the accounts of Shambhala were already ancient by that time, having survived a thousand years before ever being committed to paper. The teachings became a part of the most sacred Tibetan holy books, the *Kangyur* and the *Tengyur*. These great works are compilations of religious doctrine—including the sayings of the Buddha—that fill the same role for the Buddhists of Tibet that the Koran does for Muslims or the Bible does for Christians and Jews.

In the centuries that followed, a great many other works were produced by religious writers seeking to flesh out the descriptions in the *Kangyur* and the *Tengyur*. Folk legends about Shambhala also proliferated, including some that are alleged to be the firsthand accounts of yogis who have traveled to the mystical kingdom and returned to extol the wonders they experienced. In the view of most lamas, however, the most essential truths about Shambhala can never be written down. They can be conveyed only by word of mouth to individuals who are spiritually ready to receive them. It is widely believed to be impossible, therefore, to comprehend the written lore of Shambhala without substantial oral instruction.

A number of the old texts are guidebooks that purport to show the way to the hidden kingdom. But they are filled with a peculiar mix of geography and magic, and they do not really offer much concrete assistance. A typical passage might supply a seemingly useful bit of advice on where to cross a particular river in China, but then without missing a beat counsel the traveler to take to the air and fly over the neighboring mountains. As a result, even the most revered of the lamas are left to join in the endless rounds of speculation about where Shambhala might be.

Locations frequently mentioned in such discussions

Sacred to followers of the Bön religion that preceded Buddhism in Tibet, the elusive land of Olmolungring (below) differs only slightly from Shambhala. It is square rather than round and is built around a great mountain.

range from northern India and Sinkiang Province in western China to the little-explored mountains between the Gobi and the Takla Makan, the two great deserts of Central Asia. More distant locations also have their proponents. The Russian capital of Moscow has been cited by some, as have Siberia and even the North Pole. The guidebooks generally agree that Shambhala is north of the River Sita—probably a reference to a river in western China—but how far to the north they fail to say. And the ensuing directions grow even more hopelessly vague, marking the way with such ill-defined stopovers as the Land of Snow and the Valley of the Hermaphrodites.

If the Buddhist texts are elusive on the subject of location, their physical descriptions of Shambhala proper are very specific and, at times, even poetic. The kingdom is said to be protected by a ring of snow-covered mountains, which are alternatively described as either perpetually shrouded in mist or so remote that no one has ever set eyes on them. Inside this barrier is a second mountain range, also in the form of a circle. The interior ring is made up of the very highest peaks, and, together, the two mountain chains give the kingdom the shape of a mandala. This is the mystical circle that to the Buddhists is a symbol of the oneness that characterizes the universe.

Flanked by meditative saints and menacing demons, the kingdom of Shambhala finds shelter and seclusion behind a barrier of snow-capped peaks in this nineteenth-century Tibetan Buddhist tanka, or religious painting (left). Inside Shambhala, eight petal-shaped provinces surround a second, inner ring of mountains, within which a busy but placid-looking ruler presides over the country's regal capital, Kalapa.

According to tradition, the area between the two concentric mountain ranges is divided by rivers and hills to form eight distinct regions arranged like the petals of a lotus blossom. These regions are in turn subdivided into twelve principalities, all subservient to the king of Shambhala. The natural and cultural features of these outlying states are said to be splendid, with golden-roofed pagodas sprinkled across a gentle landscape of meadows and flowering trees. The real paradise, however, is inside the center ring, site of the royal city of Kalapa, the capital of Shambhala.

Kalapa is nestled in a valley of perfect harmony. It is an Eden-like place where birds sing, gentle breezes blow, incense fills the air, and blossoms float on the waters. According to legend, the king takes his place on a jewel-encrusted throne in a palace so luminous that not even night can dim its glory. Amid furnishings of gold, lapis lazuli, and diamond, the great monarch holds forth with unrivaled earthly power. At his command are limitless treasure, legions of attendants, and a bustling complement of ministers and generals. But there is rarely any need for the king to exercise his might, for all the citizens of his domain have everything they need, and they live in perfect contentment. The myth of Shambhala is Tibetan in its origins, but the name is from Sanskrit and means "source of happiness."

The chief occupation in this land of plenty is the study of the Kalacakra, or "Wheel of Time," a complex body of Buddhist teachings designed to confer enlightenment on initiates by helping them to master the art of meditation. For the time being, therefore, the principal duties of the king are to be keeper and teacher of the sacred Kalacakra.

Tibetan folklore predicts a succession of thirty-two heirs to the throne of Shambhala with each king ruling for about a hundred years. When the last of the heirs has ascended to power, the might and grandeur of Shambhala will be revealed to the outside world. Until that time, the way of life outside the hills and valleys of Shambhala will gradually deteriorate, as people increasingly ignore spiritual values and embrace materialism instead. Greed, dishonesty, and immorality will eventually run unchecked—or so the story goes—until the mists that cloak Shambhala are parted and the armies of the kingdom roll down from the mountains to impose on the world a more enlightened value system. The Buddhist faithful who keep this legend alive believe that the succession of monarchs is well advanced, but there is no agreement on exactly when the age of enlightenment will come to pass.

Western scholars point out that the peculiarly Tibetan form of Buddhism from which this tradition springs is an aberration to the extent that the teachings of the core religion originated in India and were shaped by a variety of cultural influences and superstitions as they made their way north. Nevertheless, belief in the Kalacakra and Shambhala have become fixtures in Tibet where they are embraced by all the main branches of Buddhism, including the Gelugpa sect presided over by the Dalai Lama. The teachings also spread, at various times, to other parts of Central Asia. Mongolia, in particular, was zealous in its embrace of the Kalacakra, and Nepal presented ready adherents. Similar ideas took root for a while in the Indian provinces of Kashmir and Bengal. But in the eleventh century, the armies of Islam swept across India, and the Muslims did their best to abolish all traces of Buddhism.

The spread of the Kalacakra and belief in Shambhala would have political ramifications, both for Eastern countries, such as Tibet and Mongolia, and for the Western nations of Russia and Great Britain, whose governments were vying for influence in Asia at the end of the nineteenth century. The Chinese preyed on these beliefs in convincing the Tibetans that both the Russians and the English were the long-predicted enemies of Buddhism who would eventually be crushed by the king of Shambhala. As a result of the Chinese propaganda, the Tibetan government did everything it could to keep the Western powers at arm's length.

Even by the turn of the century, the equation had become more complicated. A Siberian lama named Dorjieff had won the ear of the Dalai Lama and convinced him that Russia—a great power to the north—was in fact Shambhala. The Dalai Lama undertook to make friends with the czar and began lavishing gifts on him. When the British viceroy in India learned of this tilt toward his nation's adversary, he took decisive action. He dispatched an expeditionary force to the Tibetan capital at Lhasa, where the British troops demanded and received a treaty guaranteeing trade.

At this time Europeans were little aware of the concept of Shambhala, which had seeped out to the West only very slowly. In the early 1600s, Roman Catholic missionaries took it upon themselves to spread their faith to Tibet and China. Among the evangelists sent east to accomplish this work were two Portuguese priests, João Cabral and Estevão Cacella, who passed through Tibet on their way from India to China, or Cathay, as the country was then called. On the road, the two clerics heard mention of "Xembala," which they mistakenly took to be another name for Cathay. They set out to find Xembala and reached southeastern Tibet—to the monastery called Tashilumpo, seat of a powerful lama—before they realized their error. Returning to India, they sent letters

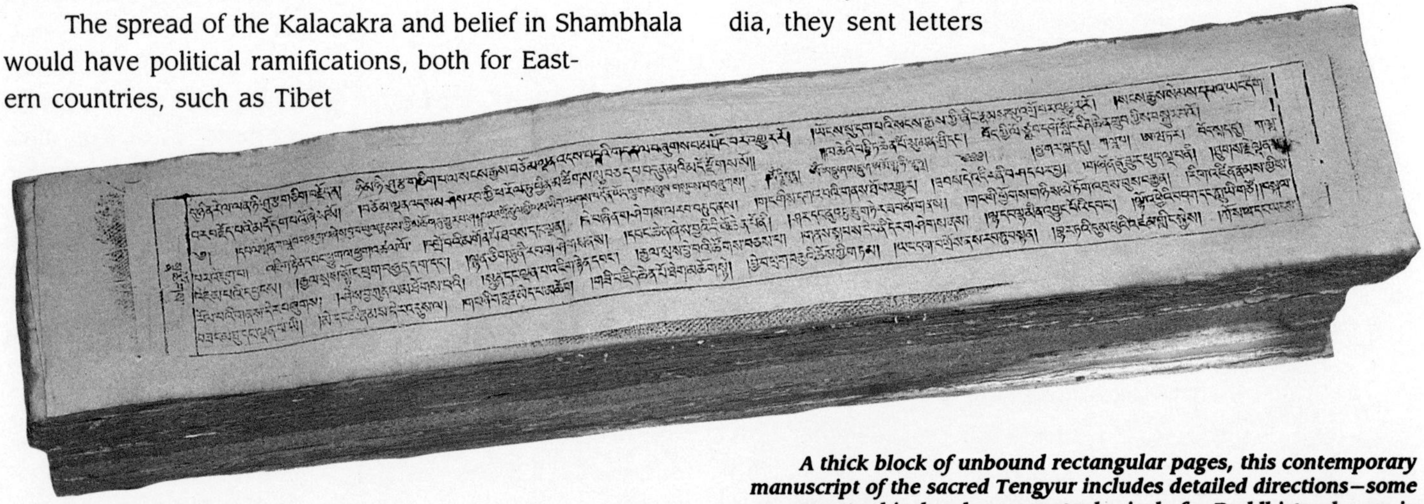

A thick block of unbound rectangular pages, this contemporary manuscript of the sacred Tengyur includes detailed directions—some geographical and some metaphysical—for Buddhists who are in search of Shambhala. Only the pure in mind should attempt the journey, warns the Tengyur, which regards unqualified seekers as "foolish children who try to reach the moon by climbing on a pile of mud."

home in which they described this aborted mission. As far as is known, their descriptions provided the first inkling in the West of the fabled kingdom of Shambhala.

Nearly two centuries later, another Roman Catholic cleric, a Frenchman named Abbé Huc, was carrying on the missionary work in Tibet when he learned the story of the hidden kingdom. His published narration of the myth would fire the imaginations of later Shambhala seekers.

A few of Abbé Huc's colleagues in Asia became deeply caught up in the religious traditions they had come to the region to uproot. One missionary in particular, a certain Father Desideri, made it his plan to learn everything he could about Tibetan Buddhism so he would be better able to refute its doctrines. He went so far as to enter a monastery in Lhasa, but his plan backfired. Father Desideri became so impressed by the devotion of his fellow monks that he could not find it in his heart to convert them. He later wrote: "I was ashamed to have a heart so hard that I did not honor my Master as this people did their deceiver."

During the first half of the nineteenth century, a Hungarian named Alexander Csoma de Koros produced the first scholarly European investigation of Shambhala. De Koros's original purpose in Asia was to discover the ancestral homeland of his people, but he wound up devoting most of his life to the study of Tibetan language and literature. On the basis of his readings of the ancient texts, he came to the conclusion that the Shambhala legend recalled a kingdom somewhere north of the Syr Darya River in territory now part of Kazakhstan. His writings, along with German translations of the Tibetan guidebooks by scholars Berthold Laufer and Albert Grünwedel, made the mystical kingdom a topic of interest to scholars in Europe and the United States.

It took the more theatrical approach of the Theosophists, however, to draw widespread attention to Shambhala. Madame Blavatsky claimed that her telepathic powers enabled her to receive long-distance communications from spiritual masters who conveyed their wisdom from somewhere beyond the Himalayas. A number of Blavatsky's followers expanded on this idea, suggesting that a sort of ultimate guru—the Lord of the World—was ensconced in an invisible garden in the Gobi Desert. They took to calling the place Shambhala.

Alexandra David-Néel, a famous and irrepressible French adventurer and writer who spent fourteen years exploring Tibet in the early 1900s, came to think of this oasis as the source of all Theosophical wisdom. Although she never actually set foot in the enchanted garden, it was, she believed, the "Holy Place where the earthly world links with the highest states of consciousness." Nikolay Roerich was the other great Theosophist explorer in Central Asia and he basically agreed with David-Néel's assessment. Roerich admitted, however, that he once had a rather discouraging conversation with a Tibetan lama, who had this to say regarding the reality of Shambhala: "Great Shambhala is far beyond the ocean. It is the mighty heavenly domain. It has nothing to do with our earth." The admonition apparently did little to discourage Roerich, who went on pursuing his vision of heaven on earth.

Western awareness of Shambhala continued to grow until 1933, when it got sidetracked—perhaps permanently—by a fictionalized takeoff on the myth that totally eclipsed the original story. That year, English writer James Hilton published his novel *Lost Horizon,* which told the story of a group of travelers lost in a plane crash, only to be rescued by the residents of a Tibetan monastery called Shangri-la. Their asylum, the travelers learned, was an extraordinary place where the residents lived for hundreds of years in peace and contemplation, engaged in the study of the collective wealth of human wisdom.

This make-believe sanctuary in the Kunlun Mountains of northern Tibet was inspired in part by the writings of Abbé Huc, and certain of the characters in the novel were based on historical figures such as Father Desideri. *Lost Horizon* had enormous appeal for readers in many countries. Its Shangri-la became synonymous with the idea of a hidden paradise, and the name was adopted by hundreds of restaurant and hotel owners around the world—all of them

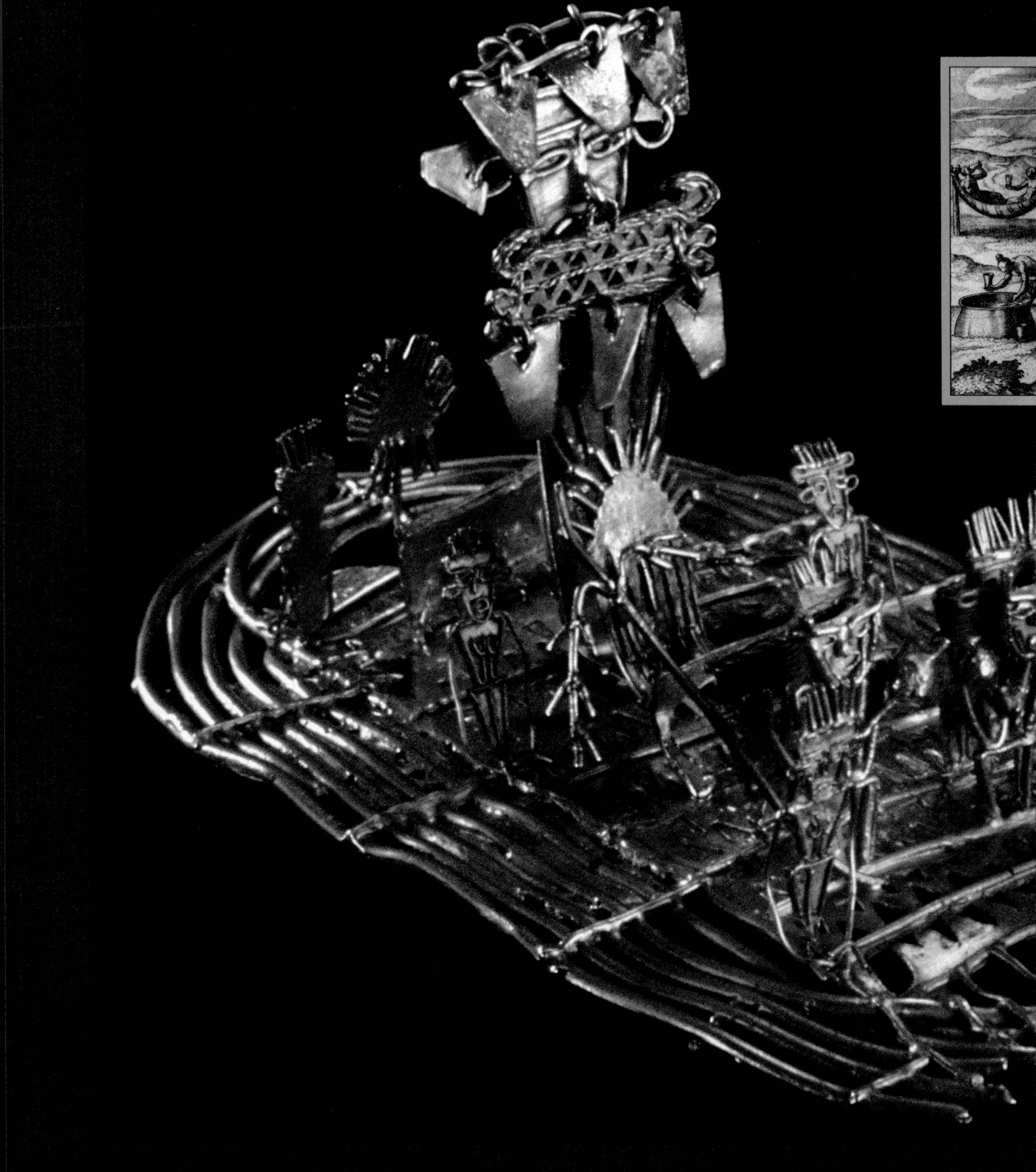

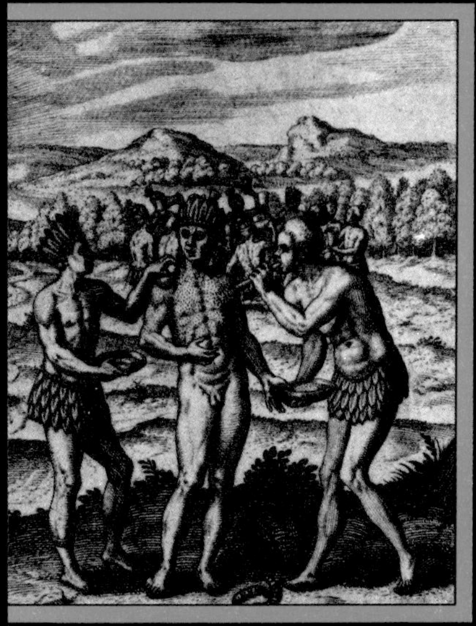

The Great Hunt for El Dorado

"The great lord or prince goes about continually covered in gold dust as fine as ground salt," wrote colonial Spanish historian Gonzalo Fernández de Oviedo in 1541. "He washes away at night what he puts on each morning, so that it is discarded and lost, and he does this every day of the year." Such tales of a wealthy Indian ruler *(inset, left),* called the Gilded One, or "El Dorado," were rife in sixteenth-century South America, where conquistadors eagerly sought local gold.

In many accounts, the golden king was linked to Lake Guatavita, north of Bogotá. Rumor had it that on ritual occasions he would dive into the lake from a barge like the one at left, losing his rich coating of powder. In the 1580s, an enterprising Spaniard drained Guatavita, killing many Indian laborers in the process. He discovered a few treasures, but no gold dust.

Meanwhile, the legend of El Dorado continued to grow. Later explorers believed El Dorado was not a man but a city or a country rich with gold. Over the next two centuries the search for this newly defined El Dorado became the grandest of treasure hunts, inspiring forays into the Andes, the Amazon basin *(below),* and the North American deserts. Yet, no trace of the golden land has ever been discovered.

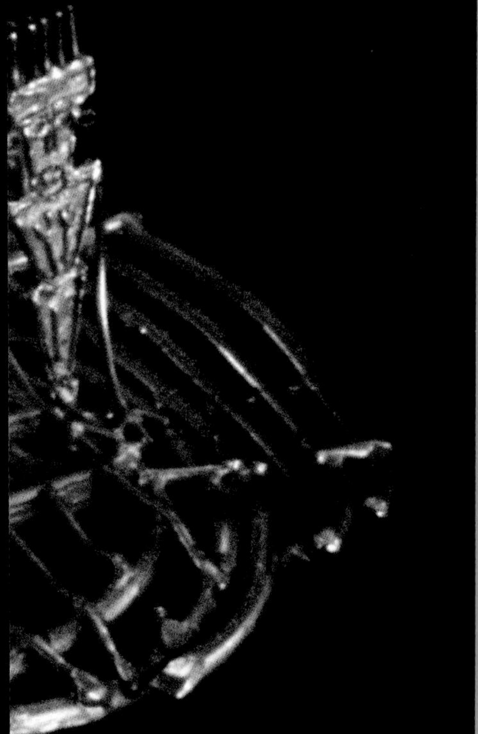

Triangle-faced figures on the tiny golden raft at left, discovered near Lake Guatavita in 1969, may represent the gold king El Dorado and his principal noblemen. In the late-sixteenth-century Spanish engraving inset above, El Dorado receives his morning powdering of gold dust from the blowpipes of two Indian courtiers.

Members of an unlikely Amazonian tribe supposedly encountered by Sir Walter Raleigh on his search for El Dorado, the headless Ewaipanoma (above) prepare for a day's hunting in this 1599 engraving. Like other seekers, Raleigh failed to locate the golden city. He had hoped to enlist its occupants in an alliance opposed to Spain.

seeking to borrow a little of the magic of the fictional heaven on earth. Ironically, Franklin Delano Roosevelt gave the name to the weekend home he had constructed for the use of future presidents in the mountains of northwest Maryland. In later years the retreat was renamed Camp David.

Perhaps the most serious and important quest for Shambhala recently undertaken by a Westerner was that of Edwin Bernbaum, an American historian who originally went to Central Asia as a Peace Corps volunteer. Bernbaum later got involved with a project to preserve old Buddhist texts, and this led to a scholarly interest in the folklore of Nepal and Tibet. As Bernbaum recalls events, he first became aware of Shambhala in 1969 while trekking through the Himalayas with a Nepalese friend, who was the abbot of a Buddhist monastery near Mount Everest. Bernbaum asked the lama half-jokingly whether he had heard of Shangri-la and went on to describe the James Hilton story. The lama pondered this account and responded that the old books speak of a place that sounded quite similar but was called by a different name.

The more Bernbaum learned about Shambhala the more amazed he became that the rich, mythological underpinnings of the Shangri-la story could have been so completely lost on his native culture. He decided to make the Tibetan myth the subject of his doctoral thesis and devoted several trips and many months to traveling through India, Nepal, and Sikkim interviewing lamas, tracking down texts, and taking pictures of artwork depicting Shambhala. Bernbaum's quest for the hidden kingdom was always that of a scholar, but he reflected on various personal experiences that shed light on the subject of his thesis.

One particular adventure that contributed to his understanding was an attempt to verify a related myth about a hidden valley in Nepal called Khembalung. Bernbaum first heard this place described as a sacred valley deep in the mountains, where devout Buddhists could meditate in a setting of bodily ease and comfort, freed from the distractions of everyday life. The stories he was told made the journey to the paradise sound extremely dangerous, however. One account made reference to snow leopards that guarded the mountain passes and would drive away any unworthy pilgrims who might be seeking Khembalung. Other stories spoke of sudden blizzards and blinding mists, and one particularly harrowing account described a party of seekers who were so terrified by their night-long encounter with a Yeti, or Abominable Snowman, that they abandoned hope of ever reaching Khembalung and made a pilgrimage to India instead.

Putting the warnings out of mind, Bernbaum decided to try to find this place, which—despite all the magical stories that surrounded it—seemed to be based on some concrete reality and bore a strong resemblance to the mythological kingdom of Shambhala. Without too much effort, he was able to lay hands on a tattered old manuscript that claimed to be a guidebook to Khembalung, and he translated it with the help of a Tibetan friend. "If you meditate in this place," read the inscription on the final page, "you will attain Nirvana in this life."

Like the word maps to Shambhala, this one was filled with bewildering descriptions of the landmarks the pilgrim would encounter along the road. One passage, for instance, pointed the way to a place that "looks like a hanging ewe's stomach." Fortunately for Bernbaum, a local lama who was familiar with the region's topography was able to make sense of even the most baroque of these characterizations and matched them up with real locations.

Bernbaum's first attempt to follow his twice-translated instructions was halted by snow cover on the high mountain passes. His second assault was a success, but not before he had undergone a harrowing journey on which one of his Sherpa guides nearly perished, and not before he was warned at every turn that no one ever returns from Khembalung alive.

The American scholar does not claim to have actually set foot in the hidden valley of Nepalese legend. Of that, he later wrote, he could never be certain. What he did find was a cleft in the great mountains that was nearly impossible to enter from above because of the ice fields and the sheer cliffs that surrounded its rim. Once entered, the valley was a place of extraordinary beauty filled with pine woods, crystal brooks, and meadows of rhododendron, all more temperate in climate than the jungles farther down through the hills.

"I felt at home and secure," Bernbaum wrote of the experience. "When we came to a glade with a spring welling out of the base of a mossy rock, I knelt to drink the water from my hands and felt the peace and beauty of the valley flow into my body. Something of it would remain, I sensed, something that I would carry back to my life outside. In coming to this place, I had touched a hidden source within myself. I had been trying to determine whether this valley was the Khembalung of the guidebook, but now that no longer mattered. I knew that this, whatever it was, was the hidden valley I had been seeking."

In retrospect, Bernbaum decided that the trip he had made did not match very closely the descriptions in the guidebook he had followed. When he mentioned this concern to the lama who had helped him comprehend the book, the priest waved aside his worries and assured him that he had indeed been to Khembalung. The discrepancies, Bernbaum was told, mattered not at all since the guidebook had been written for yogis who would have seen things very differently than he did. The American, however, took his greatest satisfaction from the intangible rewards of his visit to the valley. He was struck by the clarity of mind and feeling of wholeness he experienced there, which he knew would have been highly valued by Buddhist visitors who would regard such mental states as aids to meditation and thus helpful in attaining nirvana. It was just possible, Bernbaum believed, that places like his valley might have inspired the myths of Khembalung and Shambhala.

Underlying the stories of these hidden places was the lure of ultimate liberation from the bonds and limitations of earthly life, which is doubtless the source of the myths' appeal to Buddhists. A similar urge drove the men and women who over the millennia sought immortality through quests to quench their thirst at the Fountain of Youth or to sip an alchemist's *elixir vitae.* Facts are so intertwined with fiction in the accounts of struggles to acquire such life-sustaining tonics that it is difficult to separate the real from the imagined. Nowhere is this more apparent than in the ancient Babylonian tale of Gilgamesh, one of the world's first true mythological epics and one of the earliest stories of a quest for immortality.

The Gilgamesh myth is based on five poems dating from the second millennium BC, but the historical person who bore the name was an ancient king of Sumer who lived perhaps a thousand years earlier. He hailed from the city of Erech in the southern part of Mesopotamia and reigned sometime during the third millennium BC. Predictably enough, the Gilgamesh who survives in legend is a larger-than-life figure, part mortal and part divine. He is a demigod who knows all and rules with a fist of iron. As depicted in the poems—and also in an epic narrative that was carved on twelve stone tablets—this ruthless king meets his match in Enkidu, a giant created by the gods in response to the prayers of Gilgamesh's subjects, who are weary of their leader's tyranny. A trial of strength ensues and it ends in victory for Gilgamesh. But surprisingly, the struggle makes fast friends of the combatants.

What brute force could not achieve, friendship does, and much to the delight of the king's oppressed subjects, Gilgamesh channels his dictatorial tendencies into a newfound thirst for adventure. Together, he and Enkidu set off to prove their mettle. First they challenge Huwawa, the guardian of a fabulous cedar forest, and mow down the woodland before slaying its protector. Further adventures bring additional glory to the two comrades, but they also invite the revenge of the gods. Finally, after a dream in which Enkidu imagines himself entering a "house of dust," the king's partner falls ill and dies.

The death of his friend causes Gilgamesh to confront his own mortality. Growing more and more determined to escape death, he sets out in search of Utnapishtim, who was the survivor of a great flood that had devastated Babylonia and all the known world. Gilgamesh's steps are sped

Bearded and elaborately coiffed, the hero Gilgamesh hoists a struggling lion in this scene from an Assyrian cylinder fashioned between 1350 and 1000 BC. He defeated many wild animals, but Gilgamesh failed to vanquish death.

by his fervent hope that the wise Utnapishtim will divulge the secret of immortality.

Like all great questers of myth, however, Gilgamesh must first face a series of tests before he can achieve his goal. Mountains slow his progress and, at one narrow pass, he finds his way is blocked by a scorpion-shaped man and a woman so horrible that a glance from her eyes can bring certain death. In deference to Gilgamesh's partial divinity, he is permitted to proceed unmolested, but once past the gate this awful couple was guarding, he finds himself in a tunnel. For the next twelve hours he must fumble his way through impenetrable darkness before at last emerging into a fabulous garden.

The garden in turn leads to the seaside and to temptation at the hands of a nymph called Siduri, who reminds Gilgamesh that "when the gods made men, they saw death for men; they kept life for themselves." Better for Gilgamesh, Siduri coos, to "fill thy belly and make merry by day and night. On each day make a feast, and dance and play, day and night."

Gilgamesh finds it in himself to turn away from this temptress and beats a path to shore. From there he is ferried across the Waters of Death for his long-awaited meeting with Utnapishtim. The wise man regales Gilgamesh with the story of the great flood and tells of his own escape from death. Utnapishtim, it seems, struck a bargain with the gods but apparently holds out little hope for his disappointed listener. "Which of the gods," asks the wily old man, "will unite thee to their assembly, that thou mayest obtain the life that thou seekest?"

Aware of his own poor standing with the gods, Gilgamesh seems destined to die—the same as any other mortal. Utnapishtim, however, takes pity on the king and sets him another test. Gilgamesh's new challenge is to remain awake for six days and seven nights, thereby conquering sleep and transcending his humanity. But he no sooner undertakes Utnapishtim's test than he fails it miserably. Sleep, "like a violent wind," fells the would-be immortal, who slumbers without so much as a stir for the entire six days and seven nights during which he had hoped to stay awake. Once roused, Gilgamesh blames his failure on a demon and, in a comment that speaks to the heart of the human condition, observes: "In the room in which I sleep, death lives, and wherever I go, death is there!"

Newly resigned to his fate, Gilgamesh is about to depart when Utnapishtim takes pity on him once again. This time the wise man decides to let him in on a secret of the gods—a plant that supposedly will restore his lost youth. Nothing comes easy for Gilgamesh, however; he learns that the miraculous plant grows only on the floor of the sea. Undaunted, he leaps into the water, swims to the bottom, and scoops up great handfuls of the rejuvenating plant. But instead of swallowing the plant immediately, Gilgamesh unwisely heads for home and pauses along the road to bathe in a spring. While he is refreshing himself, a serpent slithers out of the spring and seizes the plant in its jaws. The serpent escapes, shedding its skin as it goes in a symbolic renewal of its youth. Gilgamesh, who has come so close and yet failed so completely, is left empty-handed and weeping.

In rebelling against his fate and yet succumbing to it in the end, Gilgamesh is emblematic of all that is mortal. He is Everyman, born to live and doomed to die. The myth shows that even in the earliest phase of recorded history, there is full awareness that although mountains and darkness can be conquered, although life's scorpion-men can be cowed into compliance and the waters of death safely navigated, death itself is inescapable. Even the greatest hero must eventually submit to this inevitability. The gods, as Siduri had cautioned Gilgamesh, "kept life for themselves."

Even so, Gilgamesh's failure to fulfill his quest, proof to some of the inherent futility of trying to prevail over mortality, only heightened the challenge for others. And as the human experience continued so did the search for secrets of the gods, magic potions or miracle elixirs that would unknot the noose of death, once and for all. In many cases, the magic was thought to reside in water, whether it was the alchemist's elixir vitae or what the Bible called "the river of the water of life." Other imagined sources of the rejuvenat-

ing waters were the fabled Fountain of Youth and the "well at the world's end."

Whatever its source, the water of life was deemed to hold the power to cure any and all diseases, to renew youth, to restore the dead, and to render immortal all who drank it. That water should be imagined the medium for so many blessings is not entirely surprising, since all life depends on the liquid. Indeed, as the life's blood of the earth and the wellspring of all fertility, water has long been the archetypal symbol of healing and rebirth, as well as the central ingredient in thousands of rituals. The waters of baptism, for example, are said to purify the Christian soul, much as the waters of the holy river Ganges are thought to cleanse the Hindu of spiritual impurities. Likewise, it is the pent-up water of life that Perceval looses in the legend of the Holy Grail to restore the Waste Land to fertility *(page 117)*, and certain springs in many parts of the world are places of pilgrimage because they are rumored to hold the cures to childlessness and sterility.

It was probably inevitable, therefore, that the age-old search for water would at times assume a mystical character. What is perhaps surprising is that the quest for water with supernatural powers was taken up by some of history's most notable personalities. Among them was Alexander the Great, who, it was said, journeyed to the ends of the earth in order to find the water that would give him immortality. For all his glory and fame—which were of remarkable magnitude even during his own lifetime—Alexander the Great apparently envied the gods. Ironically, he was only thirty-three years of age when he died of fever in 323 BC.

The legends that surround the figure of Alexander are as numerous as his actual conquests, and many of the stories recount the trials that marked his quest for the Well of Life. In one such tale, Alexander approaches a lake, at the center of which lies an island. On this isolated patch of land stands a castle with a gateway that is inscribed with an ominous warning: "No man may go in to the greatest and least treasure of the world until he has passed the night of fear." Puzzled by how a treasure can at once be greatest and least, but determined to find out for himself, Alexander orders his men to bed down outside the gate and prepare themselves for whatever terrors the night of fear might bring. They do not have long to wait, because soon they find themselves fighting for their lives against fearsome tigers and dragons. Other beasts join in the battle, among them powerful lions, enormous crabs, and overgrown mice and bats. All these attackers are followed by an army of six-handed men. Morning at last sees the drawbridge lowered, and Alexander and his men hurry across it to enter the castle. There, beneath a legend proclaiming "the greatest treasure and the least," they find an egg-shaped stone. They can see inside the stone everything that any man could desire in this world—everything, that is, except Alexander's magical waters of everlasting life.

Another legend puts the great conqueror on the path to the world's end, where he finds himself in a place pocked with many wells. The emperor's cook happens to dip a dried fish into one of the springs and is astonished to see the fish come to life and swim away. Greatly intrigued, the cook sips from the well and in an instant is rendered immortal. Upon learning of his cook's extraordinary good fortune, Alexander orders the man to show him to the well immediately. Eager to comply but unable to recall exactly which of the wells is the magical one, the cook only succeeds in stoking the emperor's anger. In the heat of his rage, Alexander tries repeatedly to kill the cook, forgetting that the man has been rendered immune to death. Finally, the frustrated Alexander hurls the cook into the sea to live forever as an ocean spirit.

Alexander's search for the water of life was echoed nearly 2,000 years later by the quest of a Spaniard named Juan Ponce de León. In 1493, at the age of nineteen, Ponce de León set sail with Christopher Columbus on the latter's second voyage to America. It was probably in the course of this journey that the young seaman first heard the tales about a fountain of youth with magical waters that healed the sick, rejuvenated the aged, and conferred immortality. It may also have been at this same time that Ponce de León set his mind on the goal of someday drinking from the source, which the natives of the New World referred to as the Fountain of Immortal Love.

In their tales, the Indians cited miraculous fountains at a number of different locations, but most of the stories concerned the island of Bimini in the Bahamas. At the time, many Europeans believed that the New World was the lost Garden of Eden, so some of the Indian legends even made their way into the history books. Peter Martyr d'Anghiera, for example, who wrote one of the earliest histories of the New World in 1511, noted that on Bimini there was "a spring of running water of such marvelous virtue, that the water thereof being drunk, perhaps with some diet, makes old men young again." A century later, another historian would claim that Indian chiefs were frequent visitors to the fountain, and that one old man had barely survived the journey to the fountain but was able to resume "all manly exercises . . . take a new wife and beget more children" after reviving himself in its waters. (Much, much later, in 1865, acclaimed American historian Francis Parkman was to look back on the old stories of the Fountain of Youth and credit them to the conquistadors' obsession with "the beauty of the native women, which none can resist, and which kindled the fires of youth in the veins of age.")

Apparently, the story that did the most to inspire Ponce de León's imagination was told to him by an Indian chief named Atamara. The chief recounted his people's complicated myth of creation in which the First Man and the First Woman are granted immortality by the Spirit of the Earth when they drink from the Fountain of Youth. That wondrous fountain, Atamara informed his eager listener, could be found on an island, in "a little vale encircled by gentle hills in whose center is a shining lake fed by many springs. The birds there are of

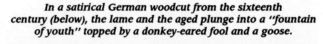

In a satirical German woodcut from the sixteenth century (below), the lame and the aged plunge into a "fountain of youth" topped by a donkey-eared fool and a goose.

Aeson, the father of the Greek hero Jason, observes as the witch Medea transforms an old ram into a lamb by means of a magic cauldron in this scene from a fifth-century-BC vase. Aeson himself is said to have been rejuvenated by a plunge into the same pot.

Changing Myth to Reality

"This treasure of the *supposed mythical* King Priam of the *mythical* heroic age, which I discovered at a great depth of the *supposed mythical Troy,*" wrote self-styled antiquary Heinrich Schliemann with heavy sarcasm after unearthing the gold and jewels shown below, is "an event that stands alone in archaeology." For Schliemann, the treasure was proof positive that the mounded Turkish ruin of Hissarlik contained the remnants of fabled Troy, the citadel besieged in Homer's eighth-century-BC epic poem, the *Iliad.*

Schliemann's barbs were directed at his contemporaries who believed that the Trojan War was pure literary invention. In spite of the prevalence of this view, popular interest in the adventure had soared in the 1800s after Greece won independence from Ottoman Turkey.

By the late 1860s, when Schliemann sought concrete evidence of Troy, he had retired from a career in business and had taken up his quest for Homer's inspiration chiefly as a labor of love. He was guided to Hissarlik by a local consul with an interest in antiquities, and he employed Turkish workmen to dig through five layers of stratified remains before identifying the second one from the bottom as the vestiges of Troy. Although other historians questioned that conclusion, for Schliemann the matter was resolved in 1873 with the discovery of the jeweled cache, which he dubbed "the Treasure of Priam" in honor of the Trojan king.

Modern archaeologists agree that Schliemann did find Troy, although the city of Homer's time was probably located one level above that of the treasures. Despite—or, perhaps, because of—his lack of formal training, Schliemann succeeded in bringing to light an ancient city that had long been banished to the never-never land of mythology.

Looking every bit the image of a prosperous nineteenth-century merchant, Heinrich Schliemann (above) concealed a romantic's heart beneath his stiff business attire. After accumulating a fortune in commercial ventures that supposedly included smuggling tea into Russia and cornering the market on saltpeter during the Crimean War, Schliemann gave up trade at the age of thirty-six to seek the lost ruins of Troy.

Taf. 204
Trésor de Priam découvert à 8½ mètres de profondeur

In the nineteenth-century photograph at left, the jewels that Schliemann linked to Troy's King Priam are displayed along with the copper salvers and cauldrons in which some of them were discovered. The treasures vanished from a Berlin museum in 1945 and were probably melted down for their gold. Rumors persist, however, that the Trojan cache found its way into the collection of a Texas oil millionaire.

At right, an ancient amphitheater unearthed since the time of Schliemann's discoveries glistens in the sun. Built by the Romans long after Homer's day, the open-air theater is typical of the large-scale structures—including temples and city walls—that Schliemann and subsequent excavators found in the vicinity of Hissarlik.

El Adelantado IUAN PONCE Des-
cubridor de la Florida

Armored for battle, a pensive Juan Ponce de León is surrounded by warlike goddesses, Indian bows and arrows, and bloody scenes of war in the eighteenth-century Spanish engraving at left. The ship behind him may be the one in which he sought the Fountain of Youth.

many colors and sing all the songs known to birds. There are many pleasant fruits and embowering vines, and flowers bloom all the year."

Not until 1513 did Ponce de León, by then one of the most powerful Spaniards in the New World and a former governor of Puerto Rico, have the chance to search for the fountain himself. He sailed past Bimini and the Bahamas on his way to Florida, which he thought to be just another island. Soon afterward, he learned from a local Indian chieftain that there was a seemingly bottomless spring located nearby in the "country of Tegesta," which was held sacred by the inhabitants of the region.

The Indian had neglected to mention the various difficulties that were involved in getting to this intriguing place, but Ponce de León and his men found that to do so they had to traverse jungles so dense as to be nearly impassable and wade through swamps infested with alligators, snakes, and other wild animals. Beyond these barriers, however, lay a pleasant, fertile land of many villages and gardens—and somewhere nearby, the Spaniards were convinced, must be the storied fountain.

Armored and on horseback, Ponce de León and his party made an odd procession as they plodded through the Florida wilderness. Eventually, they did find the spring that the chieftain had described, but they also discovered that its waters had somehow lost their powers—either that or it had never been magic to begin with.

Disappointed but not despairing, the Spaniards pressed on until they reached the village of Acuera, which had been abandoned by all but a single old man. Ignoring this straggler's obviously advanced age, Ponce de León had his Indian guide inquire about the proximity of the Fountain of Youth. "Here?" the old man exclaimed. "Do I look as if it could be here?"

As it turned out, the old man had heard the talk about a magical spring, and he passed on his vague recollection that it was probably somewhere "in the land toward the setting sun." Becoming more expansive, he claimed to have once been taken captive and hauled off to the province of Ocali. There, he had seen a woman who "was like a daughter of the sun in her beauty." She had drunk the wondrous spring waters, the old man claimed, and "from that time knew not what age was."

Such a tale could have only one effect on the explorers. They were hastening to push deeper into the Florida wilderness when they were attacked by the vanished residents of the village, who, it turned out, had fled into the neighboring woods on the approach of the Spaniards. Forced to beat a retreat, the conquistadors returned to the safety of their ships and set a southerly course, staying close to the Florida coastline. On the way, they paused to marvel at the sea of grass known today as the Everglades.

One of Ponce de León's Indian guides spoke to the leader at this point about a spring on Bimini that was said to possess healing properties. Without so much as a moment's hesitation, the explorer trimmed his sails and set a course for Bimini—or, at least, what he thought was Bimini. The party landed eventually in Central America on the Yucatán Peninsula, and, as luck would have it, they were not disappointed, in spite of their wayward course. An old woman they encountered at this latest landfall promptly led them to a fountain that was set like a gem in a small grotto. The woman told Ponce de León that, if drunk today, the waters of the spring would restore his youth in a year's time. Puzzled, the explorer asked her why she herself did not take a drink. Old age, he pointed out, had obviously caught up with her. "I was young once," came the ready reply, "and men thought much of me. But it brought me much trouble and sorrow. I am free now, nor will I drink of the water until the evening of my day comes."

Ponce de León would have nothing of such resigned philosophizing, however. He and all his men reportedly guzzled their fill of the water at once, then topped off jugs to bring home to their wives. Years later, in 1521, the explorer supposedly asked for the dregs of his jug after being grievously wounded by a Seminole arrow. If so, the water produced no miraculous effects, for according to most accounts he died shortly thereafter, his men having transported him back home to Cuba.

In the reminiscences of one of Ponce de León's companions—his trusted cleric Fray Antonio—the hero's life came to quite a different ending, however. According to the good padre, one drink of the fabulous water and both Ponce de León and his wife were restored at once to their youth. Together, the conquistador and his lady rode off into the star-strewn night, bathed in light and led, in the priest's words, by a "presence . . . that had such a heavenly beauty as the great artists give the Divine Mother." In his old age, Fray Antonio also liked to tell how Ponce de León had once experienced a vision of a heavenly "new Alhambra" over which flags flew, bugles sounded, and cannons boomed. As the monk recalled, the conquistador predicted that not yet, but one day soon, he and his wife would "ride up to that gate, I upon my black charger and she upon her white palfrey, and bid the warder give up the keys."

His story done, Fray Antonio would heave a sigh at the memory of his lost friend and leader. "I know not where the Knight has gone with the Donna Dolores, Miguel and Atamara, the chief who gave us the Legend of the Fountain; but whether or not I ever see them again, there never was a truer Knight and gentleman in all the world, than Don Juan Ponce de León . . . nor a truer lady did God ever make than the Donna Dolores."

In the decades following the death of Ponce de León, interest in the Fountain of Youth would wane, as the quest for gold supplanted the search for anything as elusive as a water of life. Lust for territory, moreover, spurred the conquest and settlement of the Americas.

Today, with all but the most remote corners of the earth fully mapped and explored, the Fountain of Youth has never been found and is generally understood to have been a figment of the collective imagination. Psychoanalyst Ruth Knipe, who wrote a book on the subject, assumed that it was an impossible dream, stating that "the water of life and the fountain of everlasting youth have not been discovered beyond the tallest mountain or across the broadest sea," as the legends had promised, and that "rationally we understand that the sacred water dwells in the imagination of human beings." And yet she recognized the great power of a myth that could move men and women to go to such lengths to make it a reality. Knipe also believes that the idea of miraculous waters "continues to be a force within the human psyche and to express itself in visions, legends, rituals and dreams."

Other myths and cherished ideas seem to exert a similar power. Through the ages, many people have sought prizes and relics to confirm the literal truth of ancient texts, both sacred and secular. Accepted wholeheartedly until the modern era, some of these documents from the past were dismissed by nineteenth-century rationalists as fairy tales—dismissed, it turned out in some cases, too soon. In the 1870s, a middle-aged German businessman and amateur archaeologist named Heinrich Schliemann bucked this trend by refusing to believe that the story of the ancient city of Troy, featured in Homer's epic poem the *Iliad,* was a myth. And Schliemann proved his case in 1872 by finding the actual remains of Troy.

Inspired by Schliemann's feat, scholars have since traced the route sailed by Homer's hero Ulysses *(pages 49-61)* and sought the origins of the poet's vortex Charybdis in the whirlpools of the Ionian Sea and the Strait of Messina. Halfway around the world, Norse sagas from the Middle Ages have guided archaeologists to old Viking settlements on Canada's northeastern shore.

The West holds no monopoly on the search for confirmation of ancient tales. In 1973, for example, determined archaeologists performed excavations in a small Indian village called Piprahwa near a site that had long been rumored to be the burial place of the Buddha. They were fortunate enough to uncover a soapstone casket inscribed in an ancient script with the name Prince Siddhārtha, which was the secular title of the great sage and religious leader. Some of the scholars who have since investigated the discovery are convinced of the inscription's authenticity, suggesting that the casket may indeed have once contained the bones of the Buddha.

Such an isolated discovery pales, however, beside the torrent of archaeological endeavor inspired by the Bible. Sacred in its various editions to the Jews, the Christians, and the Muslims, the Bible is often called the most widely read book in the world. Its most ancient passages are known to Christians as the Old Testament. They blend secular events and divine interventions in a narrative that spans about five thousand years. In the process, the scriptures name hundreds of places and describe a far greater number of occurrences, many of which pose challenges to archaeologists who are of a mind to take the words literally.

Some modern theologians contend that the Bible is not always meant to be taken in that spirit. They suggest that the Garden of Eden, for instance, never physically existed but is just a metaphor for primeval innocence, while the story of Noah's Ark is a commentary on the relationship between God and humankind. But a great many others, including conservative Protestants known as fundamentalists, take a more unequivocal view. If the Bible is indeed the word of God, they contend, it must by definition be truthful in every detail.

Over the years, a number of such believers have made it their quest to prove the literal truth of the Bible, and their fundamentalist supporters have not hesitated to put their money where their faith is. During the late 1800s and early 1900s, the vast majority of archaeological expeditions to the Holy Land were funded at least in part by devout philanthropists hoping to validate the details of one biblical story or another. Some of these projects gave rise to a specialized field of research known as biblical archaeology, an academic discipline which accepts that new discoveries may contradict the Bible. But many other people involved in this work continue to take the Bible as an infallible source of the truth. Whether searching for the Ark of the Covenant, the wealth of King Solomon, or the sinful cities of Sodom and Gomorrah, numerous excavators and explorers have tirelessly endeavored to authenticate the Bible's literal truth.

Such research is not without its share of theological critics. Biblical miracles are best taken on trust, the objectors contend, not something to be subjected to legalistic tests of evidence. Seventeenth-century British theologian Sir Thomas Browne said that to believe only that which has been proved possible "is not faith, but mere Philosophy." Yet there are many, no matter how devout, who persist in the quest for certainty, hoping that nonbelievers will be converted, and skeptics confounded, by the next verification of biblical detail.

One of the first biblical quests of modern times, however, had more to do with treasure hunters' fever than with religious zeal. Beginning in the 1800s, adventurers and other researchers scoured the Bible for clues to the source of King Solomon's riches. Renowned for his wealth as well as his wisdom, Solomon is said to have imported his treasure from rich mines in a distant country known as Ophir. Because the writers of the Bible provided few hints as to the location of this country, excavations have been launched in places as varied as Africa, Saudi Arabia, and even Peru.

Based on the reports of early Portuguese explorers, who told of finding ruins of large and complex structures in southern Africa, an 1890 expedition headed by British explorer J. Theodore Bent made extensive digs in Zimbabwe, an ancient stone city for which the modern-day African country is named. Bent's party, which inspired British author Henry Rider Haggard to write a best-selling novel called *King Solomon's Mines,* unearthed a number of fascinating African ruins. But to modern eyes, the digging did more harm than good. Bent not only failed to locate the gold mines, his excavation caused considerable damage to the site, which was of great importance to the study of African history.

In 1932, an American mining engineer named Karl Twitchell came across a considerably more plausible site while he was surveying Saudi Arabia for mineral deposits. Twitchell found traces of several ancient mines, but the richest of them by far was the Mahd adh Dhahab, or "cradle

of gold,'' located halfway between Mecca and Medina. Despite archaeological evidence of extensive mining, the Mahd adh Dhahab's remaining store of gold and silver was, according to Twitchell, ''the largest I ever saw in Arabia.'' He added that ''it is reasonable to guess that this might have been the source of King Solomon's gold.'' The mine was promptly reopened by British archaeologists, and it was operated profitably until 1954.

The United States Geological Survey and scientists employed by the Saudi Arabian government tentatively confirmed Karl Twitchell's theory in 1977, when they reexamined the Mahd adh Dhahab in yet another mining survey. Their calculations of the total amount of gold that may have been mined from the site match up well with the biblical accounts, which state that Solomon and the king of nearby Tyre imported what amounts to almost thirty-one metric tons of gold from Ophir. The Mahd adh Dhahab's proximity to ancient trade routes adds weight to the theory because it suggests that the gold could have easily been transported to Jerusalem.

Convinced that the hieroglyphics on this Peruvian boulder reveal the influence of gold-seeking envoys from the biblical kingdom of Solomon, American explorer Gene Savoy hopes to discover evidence that will overcome the skepticism of more convention-bound historians. One of the clues that he finds persuasive is that the people responsible for the writing were called Chachas, or "cloud people," because of their white skin and blue eyes, features that were very rare in pre-Columbian South America.

Meanwhile, increasing scholarly respect for the abilities of ancient Phoenician sailors has led a number of researchers in a drastically different direction. These historians suggest that the mines could have been located much farther away from Israel, in mineral-rich South America. Some controversial support of this possibility turned up in 1989 when an American explorer named Gene Savoy uncovered evidence that he believes places the mines somewhere in the wilds of Peru.

That year, while exploring a remote cave near a centuries-old Chachapoyan Indian city he had discovered, Savoy unearthed three massive stone tablets, each weighing several tons. The tablets, he said, bore ancient patterns which he identified as writing. They also included hieroglyphics similar to some he had seen on pottery fired in King Solomon's time. One of the hieroglyphics, Savoy claimed, was identical to a symbol that appeared on the ships the great king once dispatched to Ophir.

Experts in ancient Peruvian history, while acknowledging some of Savoy's contributions to their field, are highly skeptical of this interpretation. The symbols, if genuine, would suggest the existence of previously unknown trade relationships between ancient Israel and the Americas. The hieroglyphics would also mark the first samples of writing ever attributed either to the Chachapoyan Indians or to the Incas who inhabited the region in King Solomon's time—the tenth century BC.

If scholars remain uncertain of even the continent that supplied King Solomon's wealth, they are in full agreement about the general location of several other biblical sites, including the vanished cities of Sodom and Gomorrah. Two of the five so-called Cities of the Plain, Sodom and Gomorrah were said by the Bible to have been destroyed by God for the many sins of their residents. Geographical allusions make it clear that all five cities were situated somewhere near the Dead Sea.

In 1960, an American minister and scuba-diving enthusiast named Ralph Baney took that biblical reference to its logical conclusion when he searched for the twin cities not near, but under, the Dead Sea. After securing the sponsorship of Jordan's King Hussein, Baney and his team used sonar equipment to chart the bottom of that body of water and then descended to the likeliest undersea locales.

The diving was extremely hazardous. The Dead Sea's silty floor lies in utter darkness as much as 200 feet beneath the surface. Its water has the highest saline content of any sea or lake in the world—about seven times greater than that of ordinary ocean water. Nauseating if not actually toxic when ingested, the Dead Sea water renders everything in it extremely buoyant. Just to sink below the surface, Baney had to carry 228 pounds of equipment, including an 80-pound block of solid lead.

Overcoming these and other obstacles, including the skepticism of several of his royal advisers, the Kansas City minister eventually turned up what he believed to be a roadway beneath a shallow section of the Dead Sea at its southern end. The discovery convinced Baney that Sodom or Gomorrah may have been at that location. "This could very well have been a large plain in Biblical days," he wrote in 1962. "The volcanic eruptions and other God-sent manifestations of His wrath apparently caused the Dead Sea waters to rise and cover these lost cities."

Unfortunately for Baney, his theory was disproved in 1979, when irrigation demands on the Jordan River led to a drop in the water level that exposed much of the southern Dead Sea bottom. Archaeologists Walter Rast of Valparaiso University in Indiana and Thomas Schaub of Indiana University in Pennsylvania concluded that the uncovered plain had been uninhabited from at least 3000 BC, a thousand years before Sodom and Gomorrah had their sinful day.

Rast and Schaub had earlier begun excavating five Bronze Age sites near the south end of the Dead Sea. The number, location, and age of the sites, according to the two archaeologists, suggest that they may be all that remain of the Cities of the Plain. Significantly, at least one of the ruins appears to have been destroyed in a catastrophic fire.

While some biblical explorers have searched for lost

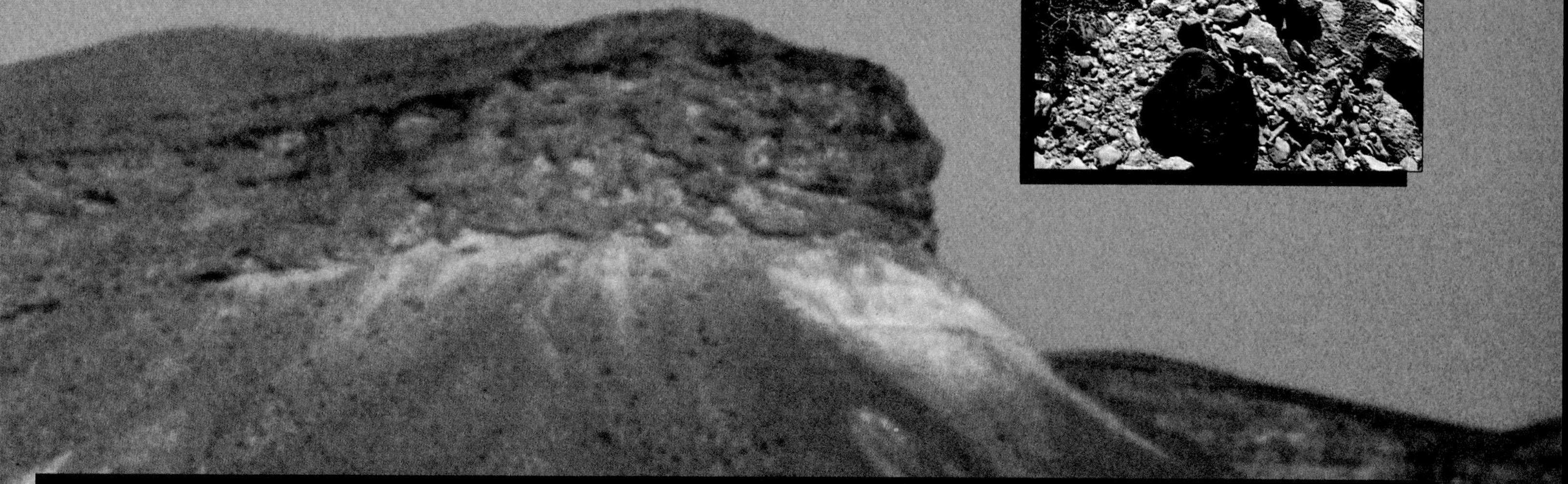

Dark, image-laden rocks line a path to the summit of Har Karkom, one of two such trails discovered by Emmanuel Anati. Among the pictographs found on the mesa were hunting scenes from the fourth millennium BC and more abstract images—some of them possibly depicting worship—from the subsequent Bronze Age.

Seeking God's Footprints

Perhaps the most sacred mountain in Judeo-Christian tradition, Mount Sinai is the place where God spoke to Moses from a fiery cloud and inscribed the Ten Commandments on twin tablets of stone. Over time, however, the precise locale of these events has become a matter of uncertainty. Scholars can only speculate that the peak lies in the eastern part of Egypt's Sinai Peninsula.

A novel alternative to this view, put forward in 1985 by Italian archaeologist Emmanuel Anati, locates the mountain some distance away in Israel's Negev Desert, four miles from the Egyptian border. There, on a low but dramatic mesa named Har Karkom *(background),* Anati has identified hundreds of apparently religious images like the one at right, as well as rock formations that, he suggests, may have served as altars or temples.

Other researchers are unimpressed by Anati's theory, in part because he dates the rock drawings to a period 1,500 years before the time of Moses. According to the mainstream scholarly view, the images on Har Karkom are more likely the work of bored shepherds, who were drawn there not by any sacred impulse, but by the plentiful water that it offered their flocks.

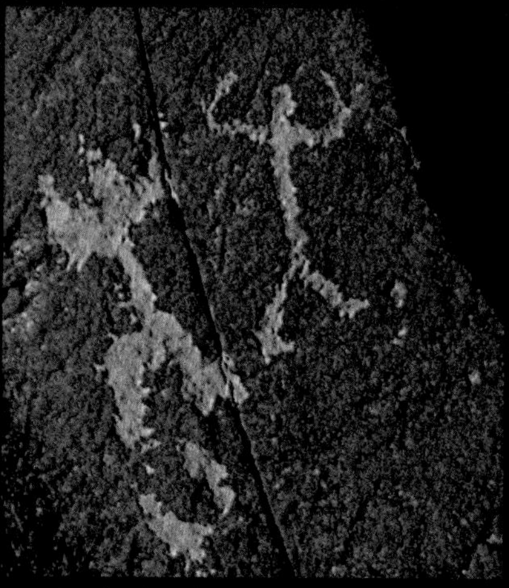

Arms raised and heads held high, two ancient figures in what Emmanuel Anati considers to be a prayerful posture ornament a stone on Israel's Har Karkom.

mines and vanished cities, others have sought the very symbol of the ancient Israelite nation—the Ark of the Covenant that was created according to instructions God gave Moses. As recounted in the Book of Exodus, the ark was a footed chest made of acacia wood, about four feet long, two feet wide, and two feet high, and plated with pure gold. It was carried on two gold-plated poles inserted through four gold rings fastened to its four feet. The ark held the Ten Commandments and other sacred Hebrew writings. To the Jews, this chest represented the presence of their God among his chosen people, and it was believed to actually house God's spirit on certain occasions. So potent was this emblem of the Jewish nation, wrote American explorer Antonia Futterer in 1927, that its rediscovery would "shake the world." Finding the ark, Futterer wrote, would "change the belief of millions of people of all nations for the better; be the greatest blow skeptics ever received; and perhaps be the greatest modern proof of the authenticity of Holy Writ."

Futterer's personal expeditions to Mount Pisgah, in the vicinity of the Dead Sea, failed to locate the Ark of the Covenant, but his enthusiasm for the project infected many others with ark-quest fever. Generations later, an American

Lackeys in oddly medieval-looking garb transport the biblical Ark of the Covenant in this detail from an illuminated twelfth-century Bible, housed at the Church of St. Mary and the Martyrs in Rome. To the left of the bearers, Israelite leaders in classical Roman cloaks and togas observe the passage of the holy chest, which vanished in the sixth century BC. To date, all attempts to recover the Ark of the Covenant have failed.

adventurer named Tom Crotser cited the old explorer when he announced that he had not only located, but also photographed, the Ark of the Covenant during a secret 1981 dig in Jordanian territory.

From the beginning, the timing of Crotser's claim was regarded with suspicion. Earlier that summer, an American film studio had released a popular motion picture called *Raiders of the Lost Ark,* which played out the fictional story of a search for the biblical ark. Claims of an actual discovery, therefore, were bound to attract abundant coverage in the world media. The skeptics grew all the more vocal when it was revealed that Crotser had previously claimed to have found several other biblical relics, including Noah's Ark, the Tower of Babel, the city of Adam, and the stone used by Cain to kill his brother Abel.

What little credibility Crotser possessed evaporated when he announced that he would not show his photographic evidence to anyone except David Rothschild—quite a peculiar decision in light of the fact that he had never met the prominent international banker. When Rothschild showed no interest in such a meeting, Crotser relented and revealed a dozen color images to Siegfried Horn, an authority on biblical archaeology. According to Horn, ten of the twelve photographs were completely blank. The other two did show a golden box, but with what turned out for Crotser to be disastrous clarity. Analyzing the pictures, Horn detected nailheads and machined patterns on the surface of the chest that were, in his opinion, of obvious twentieth-century origin.

Furious about this unauthorized excavation and the spurious claims that stemmed from it, the government of Jordan retracted its previously extended permission for a major scientific expedition in 1982 by a party unrelated to Crotser. Meanwhile, the real Ark of the Covenant—if it still exists—eludes professional archaeologists and amateurs alike. Perhaps it will someday be discovered by pure chance rather than by design—as was a golden calf in June 1990.

The calf came to light during a routine excavation by a Harvard University team in the ancient port city of Ashqelon, west of Jerusalem in modern Israel. Rachel Stark, a twenty-year-old volunteer, was helping to unearth an ancient temple razed in 1550 BC when she uncovered a strange pottery container, roughly the size of a football. Inside was a tiny metallic figure in the shape of a calf.

Lawrence Stager, director of the dig and head of Harvard's Semitic Museum, soon announced that Stark had come across a so-called golden calf, a pagan object of worship that turns up frequently in biblical stories dating from the thirteenth through the eighth centuries BC. In the most famous instance, described in the Book of Exodus, Moses was said to have returned from Mount Sinai with the Ten Commandments only to find his fellow Israelites engaged in the worship of a golden calf. Flying into a rage, Moses destroyed the false idol.

The Ashqelon calf was small enough to fit in its discoverer's hand; it weighed less than a pound and stood only four and a quarter inches high. The tiny sculpture contained no real gold, only silver, copper, and bronze. But the silver made it the earliest known object of worship to incorporate a precious metal of any kind. Burnishing marks suggest it was polished to a high sheen, which may have given it the look of gold.

For biblical purists, golden calves, ancient cities, and, particularly, the so-far-elusive Ark of the Covenant are compelling prizes and valued pieces of evidence in support of their religious views. But even such treasures can offer only limited satisfaction, because they can all be explained in purely secular or scientific terms. The ultimate proof of the Bible's literal truth would be definitive evidence substantiating one of the many miracles that are described in scripture. To the minds of many researchers, the episode of divine intervention that was most likely to have left behind such evidence is none other than the great Flood. As a result, the search for Noah's Ark, the ship in which humanity is said to have ridden out a threat to its continued existence, has been a quest to end all quests, firing the minds of pilgrims for centuries.

The earliest known example of a calf idol like those mentioned in the Bible, the ceramic and metallic sculpture below is just four inches high. Dating from about 1550 BC, the figurine confirms that peoples of the biblical lands worshiped such images.

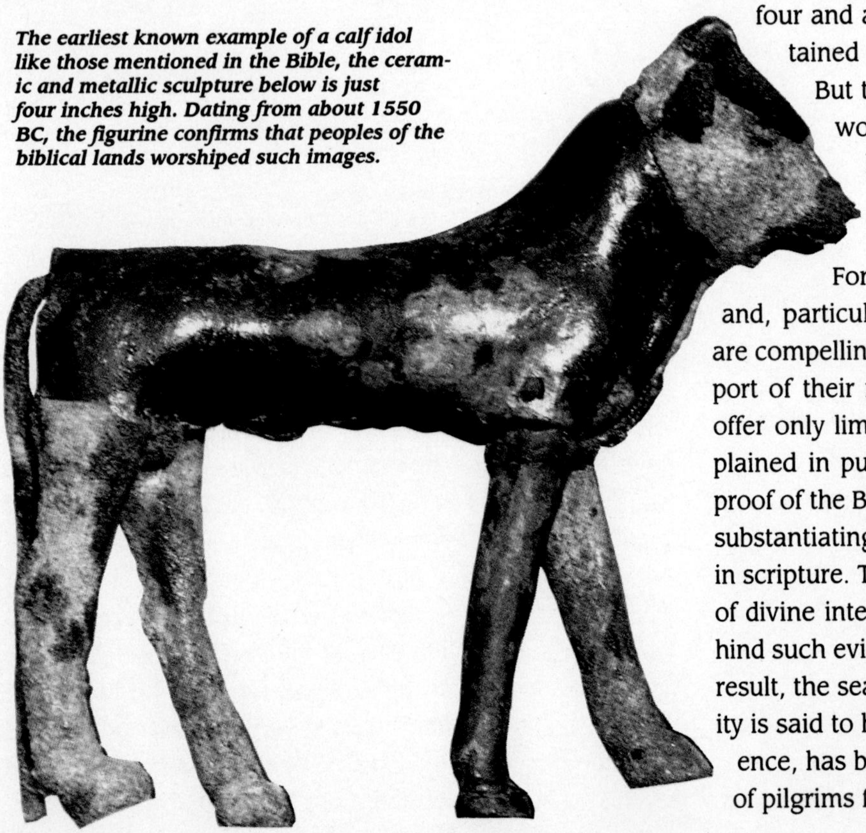

Following the Wake of Ulysses

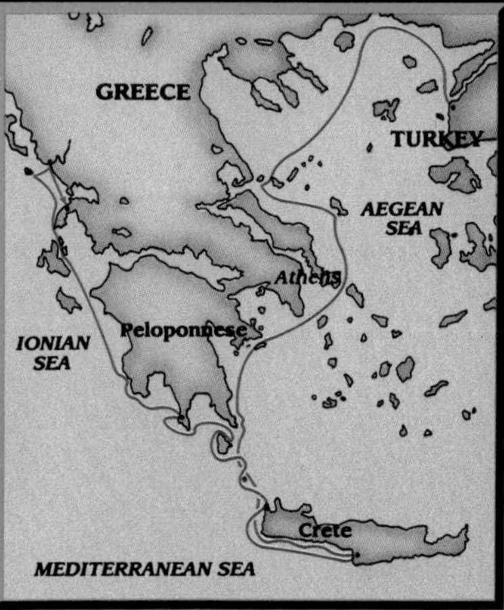

One of the best-known episodes in classical mythology is the tale of the Trojan Horse—a wooden figure of a warrior's steed that helped the Greeks breach the walls of Troy. For Ulysses, inventor of this stratagem, the adventures were only beginning. The wily general from Ithaca began a tortuous journey home. His ten-year quest was chronicled in Homer's epic poem the *Odyssey,* a narrative so full of supernatural events that it—like the story of Troy—was long assumed to be fantasy.

Then came Heinrich Schliemann, a German archaeologist whose 1870s discovery of the ruins of Troy forced historians to abandon their assumptions *(pages 36-37).* Certainly, no one rushed to embrace such obvious inventions as the one-eyed Cyclops who terrorized Ulysses or the witch-goddess Circe who turned sailors into swine. But there was suddenly reason to seriously consider that someone like Ulysses *(pictured above, left)* had commanded Greek armies and may have experienced such an arduous trip.

One scholar who attempted to come to grips with the historical Ulysses was Irish explorer Tim Severin *(above, right).* His investigatory technique was to retrace the voyage from the Dardanelles to Ithaca in a replica of a Bronze Age galley. Along the way he watched for corresponding details in Homer's descriptions, in the geology of the places Ulysses would have seen, and in the folklore preserved at those locations. Severin's quest is charted on the pages that follow; his sea route is displayed on the map above.

From a port near Troy, Severin sailed northwest to Maronia, the probable site of Ismarus—a city Ulysses is said to have sacked to reprovision his twelve-ship fleet. The historian proceeded in short hops along the coast to Cape Sounion (right), the first notable landmark of the hero's journey. Severin's navigation was based on the style of Bronze Age seafarers: Respectful of gales, the captains of that era moved cautiously from one headland to the next, waiting for the favorable wind and never intentionally losing sight of land.

In spite of such measures, the Odyssey reveals, Ulysses' fleet fell prey to the weather at Cape Malea. As the ships attempted to round the Peloponnese, they were caught in the grip of "accursed winds" and drifted for many days, winding up in the "land of the Lotus-eaters." Severin took this to be Homer's lyrical name for the little-known regions of North Africa. Unable to obtain visas from the Libyan government, he decided to forgo the extended detour.

As the sun dips toward the horizon, Severin's galley, named Argo, rounds Cape Sounion in 1985. The bold headland is crowned by the monumental ruins of a temple that was constructed in the fifth century BC to honor the sea god Poseidon.

Argo crew member Rick Williams heats the end of a gnarled tree root, repeating a famous scene from the Odyssey in which Ulysses and his men strike back at the Cyclops, who has taken them captive. According to Homer's verse, the monster had begun to eat the Greek warriors, two by two. But Ulysses had his men place an olive-wood stake in the fire and then hurled it into the Cyclops's eye, leaving him blind.

When Ulysses returned to Greece, he landed, in Homer's words, on "a luxuriant island, covered with woods, home to innumerable goats." Severin regarded this as a reference to Crete, the island nearest the African coast and a place long associated with goats. Having ventured this guess, he set out to explore the roots of the Cyclops myth in observance of Ulysses' next great trial.

Combing the southwestern coast of the island, Severin heard folklore about local bogeymen called triamates, very tall cannibals with third eyes on the backs of their heads. The more Severin listened to the legends of these ogres, the more he was convinced that they had provided the basis for Homer's monster story. Villagers had already made the same connection, identifying a slew of gloomy caves in the hills as former homes of the Cyclops.

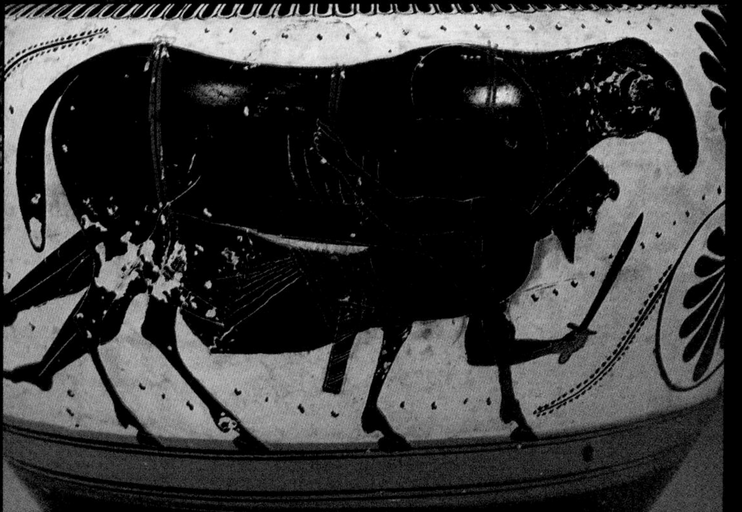

As depicted on a ceramic jar from the sixth century BC, Ulysses and his remaining comrades made good their escape by clinging to the undersides of the Cyclops's sheep when the giant put his flocks out to pasture. The sightless monster stroked the back of each animal as it passed by him, but he failed to detect his tormentors. Many Greek and Roman artifacts feature scenes of Ulysses' many adventures.

The Argo skirts the coast of Grabousa, where Ulysses waited out a gale. "All around this island," the hero noted, "there runs an unbroken wall of bronze and below it the cliffs rise sheer from the sea."

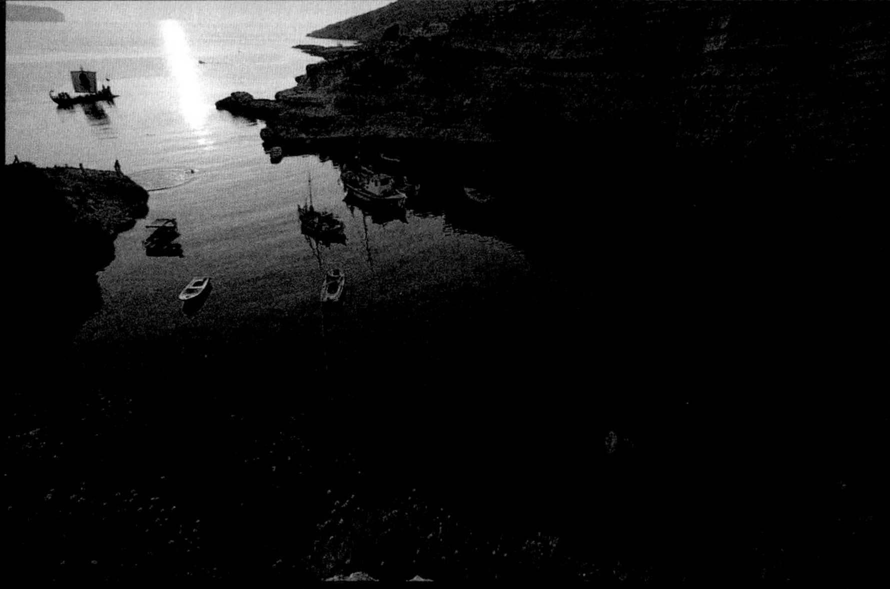

The Argo drifts past the cozy anchorage at Mezapos, where Ulysses probably watched as his fleet was destroyed. With its precipitous walls and narrow entry, the harbor neatly matches Homer's descriptions.

Delivered of the Cyclops, Ulysses and his followers attempted to cross to the mainland but were driven back by a meltemi—one of the seasonal winds that plague navigation on the Greek sea channels. For the next month, the travelers had to cool their heels in port as the guests of Aeolus, Ruler of the Winds. In keeping with the fanciful nature of the Odyssey, they could not sail on until their host had trapped the opposing winds in a leather bag.

In tiny Grabousa, northwest of Crete, Severin found an island that may have inspired the Aeolus episode. An older name for the place was Korykos, or "leather bag," and its towering cliffs closely matched those described in Homer's work. In Mezapos (above), Severin found a likely setting for Ulysses' next great crisis, the decimation of his fleet by the Laestrygones.

As depicted in a Roman mural, the pirates of Mezapos smashed eleven of Ulysses' ships, bombarding them with boulders from above. Only the hero's vessel survived.

Flares light an eighteenth-century church that is built atop the ancient Necromanteion, or Oracle of the Dead, on the Acheron River. Severin associates this site with the Halls of Hades, which are mentioned by Circe in the Odyssey.

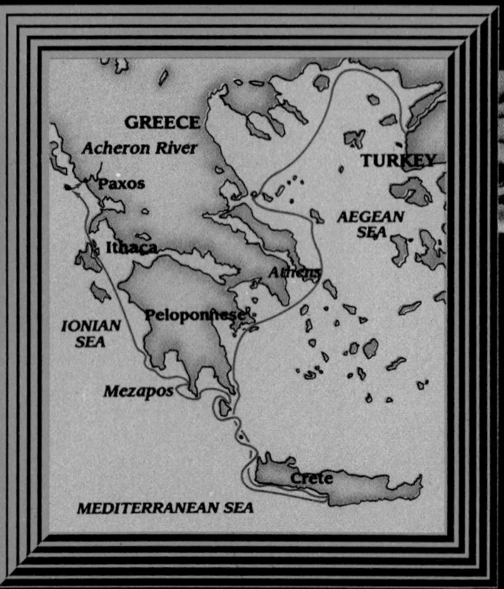

By the time Ulysses encounters the goddess Circe, who becomes his lover and ally, there is a breakdown in the logic of the Odyssey as the story of a warrior returning home. Homer permits his hero to sail right past Ithaca and then folds the folklore of western Greece into his panoramic narrative.

Ulysses lingers for a year with Circe, who had initially greeted him with scorn and sorcery (top right). Severin guessed that the small isle of Paxos may have been imagined as the background to the romance that ensues. Paxos was, he noted, a seductive patch of ground with a single freshwater spring—the kind of place "legend would locate a fairy figure like Circe."

To arrive at this theory on the geography of myth, Severin worked backward from other educated guesses about locations referred to in the Odyssey. His best clue was that Paxos was a single day's sail from the mouth of the Acheron River—a locale associated with the underworld in mythology and thus related to Ulysses' search for a ghostly Theban seer.

On an urn dating from 450 BC, Ulysses threatens Circe, and she drops the potion she had used to turn half his crew into animals. Ulysses warded off such spells by eating a plant called moly, a precaution advised by the deity Hermes.

The legend of the half-goat, half-human Pan has been associated with Paxos since classical times and may have influenced Homer's portrayal of Circe. Both deities commanded the allegiance of wood nymphs and wild creatures.

Severin was the first to link this tunnel on Sesola Island with the Roving Rocks of Homer's epic. The formation was probably the product of volcanic activity, so Circe may not have been far wrong when she said that it was "licked up by tempestuous and destroying flames."

An elderly Greek villager lights a devotional candle in a centurie old chapel, built—Tim Severin believes—in the cave of Homer's drag lady Scylla. The site of this cavern is a hill called Lamia, nam for another long-necked monster who was perhaps related to Scyl

The side of an old Greek vase shows the thorough precautions Ulysses took to see his ship safely past the land of the Sirens, where women sang with such incredible sweetness that sailors often lingered till they died. Ulysses had his crew block their ears with wax, but he insisted on hearing the music himself—all the while firmly tethered to the mast.

Circe warned Ulysses that the final leg of his journey would be filled with peril. In addition to eluding the Sirens, he would have to choose between two dangerous sea routes. One would take him past the Roving Rocks, which smashed ships to splinters. The alternative was to run a narrow channel between a boat-eating vortex called Charybdis and the seaside lair of a sea nymph who had been transformed into an awful six-headed monster named Scylla.

Severin found hints of these fanciful tales on the coastal waters between Paxos and Ithaca. Not far from the Acheron River, a small spit of land carried the name of the fearsome Scylla. As Severin sailed in that direction, he spied a desolate island marked at one end by a towering portal that was a dead ringer for the Roving Rocks (far left). If Sesola, as the place was called, marked the open-sea route to Ithaca, then the channel between the island of Leukas and the mainland was probably the alternative. Along this route Severin saw historical evidence of both a dangerous whirlpool, caused by tidal flows, and a mythical beast called the lamia, who bore strong resemblances to Scylla.

The Argo survived several sudden squalls, which in some parts of the Aegean can turn a calm sea into a raging tempest in little more than a minute. Just such a storm, Severin believes, may have cost Ulysses his final ship and the lives of his remaining comrades. In classical Greek literature, however, such a disaster is never left without supernatural explanations, and in this case the shipwreck was blamed on Zeus, who was angry at the Greeks for slaughtering a herd of sacred cattle. The image of seafaring tragedy at left dates from the eighth century BC. It may be a rendering of the Ulysses myth; if so, it is one of the very oldest known.

Severin's journey, like Ulysses', ended near the island of Ithaca, shown above at the isthmus of Aetos, where Heinrich Schliemann once searched for the hero's home. The re-created voyage lasted three months, time enough to locate many of the sites that gave shape and texture to Homer's masterpiece. According to the verse, Ulysses returned in the twentieth year, having spent ten years in the siege of Troy. When at last he presented himself to his wife, he did so disguised as a beggar. He waited to reveal his identity until after he had slain the many would-be kings who had sought her hand in his absence. A terra-cotta sculpture from the fifth century BC depicts the reunion (right).

CHAPTER 2

The Search for Noah's Ark

High atop the icy slopes of Mount Ararat in eastern Turkey, freezing winds blasted across the face of a solitary climber, bringing him momentarily to a halt. It was August 25, 1982, and James Benson Irwin shifted the weight of his pack and pressed on across the snow-covered terrain. Rugged landscapes were nothing new to this particular climber. Eleven years earlier, as an American astronaut on the Apollo 15 mission, Colonel Irwin had stood upon the cratered surface of the moon.

In many ways, the former astronaut's expedition to Mount Ararat was no less extraordinary. Irwin had laid the groundwork shortly after his return from outer space, when he established the evangelical High Flight Foundation. As a devout Christian newly inspired by his lunar voyage, Irwin intended High Flight to help him arrange lecture tours on spaceflight and on the moral values that help people "reach the heights." In time, the organization would sponsor a more unusual endeavor: a series of expeditions, beginning with the 1982 climb, to Ararat's windswept northeast side. There, Irwin and his colleagues believed, lay a bulky wooden structure abandoned almost 4,400 years before. The object they sought was nothing less than the petrified skeleton of Noah's Ark.

The High Flight team had reason to believe that the ark was to be found on Ararat; for centuries, travelers ranging from mountaineers to modern military pilots have reported catching glimpses of a giant ship in the area, and a few have even returned with what they call pieces of its wood. Yet the 1982 expedition reached the summit of the mountain without locating so much as a trace of the ark of Noah. Exhausted, Irwin had separated from the climbing party to return to base camp alone.

Suddenly, disaster struck. Cutting across a snowy slope at an altitude of about 12,500 feet, Irwin abruptly lost consciousness, apparently knocked out by a falling rock. When he regained his senses sometime later, he found himself lying in a field of jagged rocks and boulders, his body covered with cuts and bruises. As he struggled to move, the former astronaut knew at once that he was in desperate straits. His head throbbed with the pain of several deep cuts and the sharp agony of four broken teeth. Blood poured from his wounds. Grimly, Irwin decided he was in no condition to continue his descent.

As night fell and the temperature on the mountain began to plummet, Irwin crawled under a protective outcrop of rock, where he struggled into his sleeping bag. After a sleepless night, he was found the next morning by his colleagues and was hurried—by horse, car, ambulance, and finally helicopter—to a Turkish hospital.

Colonel Irwin's injuries did little to dampen his enthusiasm, nor was he daunted by the expedition's failure to discover any sign of Noah's Ark. Immediately upon his release from the hospital, Irwin began planning another assault on Mount Ararat to resume his search for the ancient vessel. After all, said the former astronaut, "God walking on the earth is more important than man walking on the moon."

Irwin, who died in 1991 after several assaults on the mountain, was not alone in his quest. Since ancient times, adventurers, holy men, and others have sought the lost ship on Ararat and on other mountains. Their motives have reflected the eras in which they lived. Two millennia ago, people were drawn to the ark by the rumored magic of its materials; in medieval times, they came as pilgrims. On at least one occasion in the 1800s, the ark served as a lighthearted rationale for British mountaineering. Some twentieth-century ark seekers, fascinated by strange and unexplained phenomena, believe the stranded ship could be evidence of an ocean cataclysm that eons ago destroyed an advanced civilization—like that of the fabled Atlantis.

But most contemporary ark researchers are fundamentalist Christians who seek the ship for still another reason: By finding it, they hope to prove the literal truth of one of the Bible's most fantastic passages. If only they can locate a ship on Ararat, they reason, even the most skeptical commentator would have to acknowledge the reality of at least one biblical miracle—or else come up with a plausible alternative explanation of how a large oceangoing vessel wound up tens of thousands of feet above sea level.

If the ruins of Noah's Ark still survive, one might think they would be hard to overlook. The Book of Genesis suggests something on the order of a gigantic floating box half as long as the luxury ocean liner *Queen Mary.* The given dimensions, when all those cubits are translated into modern terms, describe a vessel 75 feet wide, 45 feet high, and an astounding 450 feet long. Such an ungainly craft would be rather unseaworthy, say many skeptics. They also argue that even a vessel of that size could not possibly have provided food and living space for all the animals involved, which proponents of the ark quest put at about forty thousand, while others suggest the number would have been closer to four million.

Against such logical objections

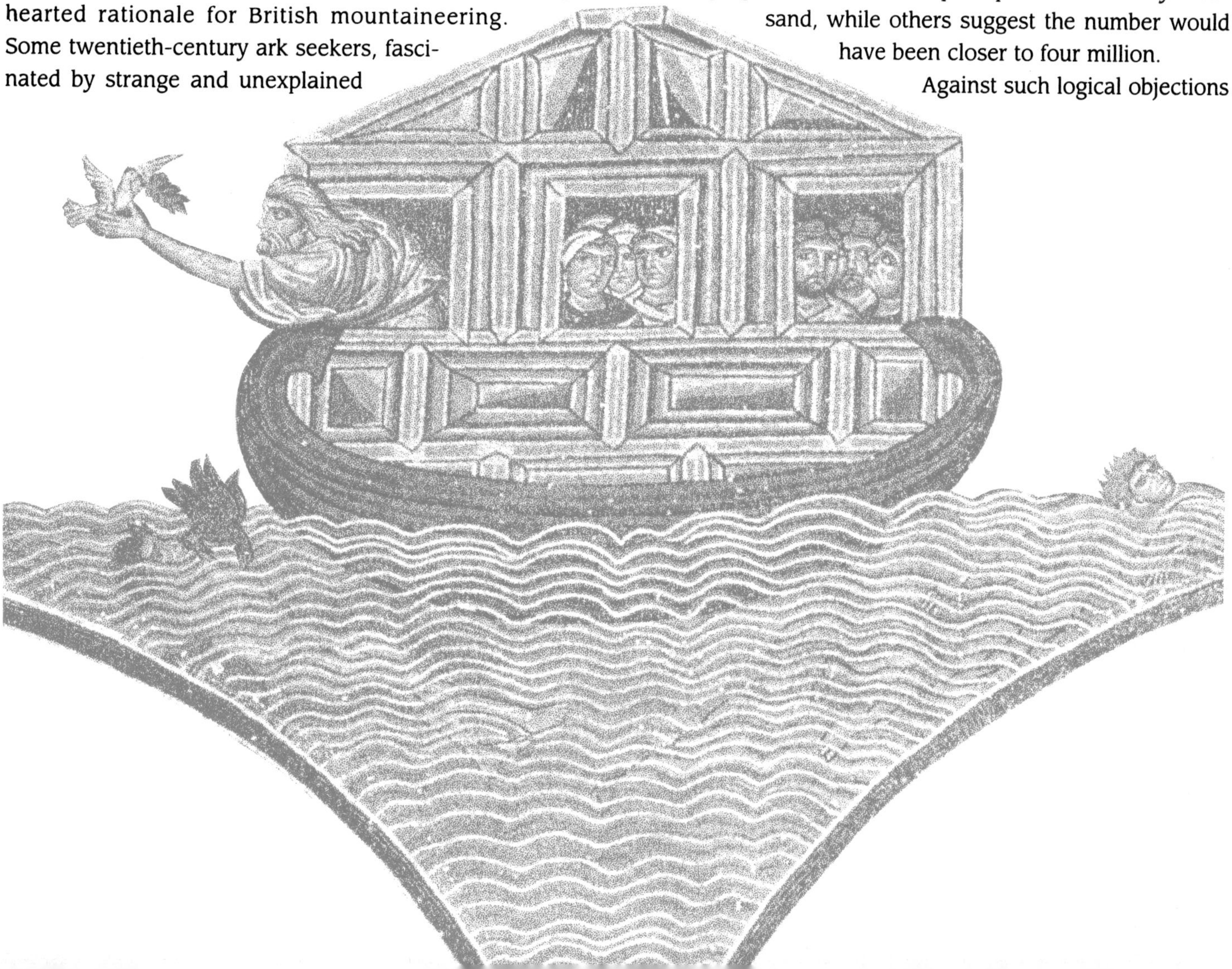

Former Apollo astronaut James Irwin, injured by a falling rock, clings weakly to the horse carrying him down Mount Ararat. Explorers seeking Noah's Ark on the treacherous peak have confronted such obstacles as rock slides, hailstorms, fierce Kurdish sheepdogs, vipers, bandits, and terrorists.

stands a wealth of suggestive evidence accumulated over the years. Several mountain climbers have reported a large wooden structure frozen into the glacial ice on Ararat with dimensions that roughly correspond to those given in the Bible. Photographs said by ark researchers to show this object have been taken from the ground, the air, and even, once, from an orbiting satellite—NASA's Earth Resources Technical Satellite, which in 1972 produced an image that, greatly magnified, appears to show a dark, ark-shaped spot. In a handful of cases, wood supposedly taken from the ark has been recovered and submitted to scientific testing, with disappointing results. In every instance, the trail has stopped short of final proof.

The Book of Genesis places the story of the ark, one of the best known of all biblical tales, just eight generations after the creation of Adam and Eve. At that time, according to the Genesis account, God became weary of humanity's many sins and decided to send a flood that would destroy nearly all life on earth. Among human beings, only Noah, a virtuous man who "found grace in the eyes of the Lord," would be spared, along with his family. Among the animals, only representative breeding pairs would be saved, to repopulate the earth after the waters receded. As a way of preserving these few creatures during the Flood, God instructed Noah to build a huge vessel—an ark—in which to house his own family and at least one male and female of each of the earth's animal species.

Make thee an ark of gopher wood," runs the divine command recorded in Genesis. "Rooms shalt thou make in the ark, and shalt pitch it within and without with pitch. And this is the fashion which thou shalt make it of: The length of the ark shall be three hundred cubits, the breadth of it fifty cubits, and the height of it thirty cubits. A window shalt thou make to the ark, and in a cubit shalt thou finish it above; and the door of the ark shalt thou set in the side thereof; with lower, second and third stories shalt thou make it."

Once Noah completed and loaded his vessel, the story continues, torrential rains began and the waters poured forth. Tending the animals, Noah and his family drifted on the world-enveloping ocean for five months, the only human beings left on earth. When the waters receded, the ship came to rest on a rocky peak. Then, says the Bible, God made a covenant with Noah never again to destroy humankind by flood, sealing the bargain with a rainbow.

Noah's story is not unique. Folklorists have found dozens of ancient flood tales around the world, from Mexico to China. According to conventional academic theory, some versions of the story are based on earlier legends. Most biblical scholars believe that the Genesis version, as well as a remarkably similar Assyrian myth, can be traced to a much earlier Sumerian story. In all three accounts, one man and his family survive a great flood by living aboard a ship that comes to ground on a mountain. In each case, the family makes sure the flood has truly receded by releasing birds that do not return.

For a time, archaeologists attributed all three stories to distant recollections of Middle Eastern floods. That theory had its origins in a discovery in 1929 by British archaeologist Leonard Wooley, who excavated the ancient city of Ur, where Abraham is said to have been born. Below several layers of broken artifacts, Wooley was stunned to find what he believed to be a stratum of river mud eight feet thick. He and his wife, Katherine, concluded that the extraordinary deluge must have been the basis for the Genesis story, since the flood would have filled the river basin that was, in effect, the entire world of those who lived there.

Later excavations in the area, however, failed to bear out that idea. A lack of mud from the same period at other sites showed that Wooley's flood did not fill the valley; it did not even cover all of Ur. But archaeological theories about the world's flood stories persist. One of several contends that such tales may reflect a truly ancient series of calamities—colossal flows from the melting of Ice Age glaciers in about the eleventh millennium BC.

That suggestion makes little impression on modern ark seekers, most of whom take a more straightforward

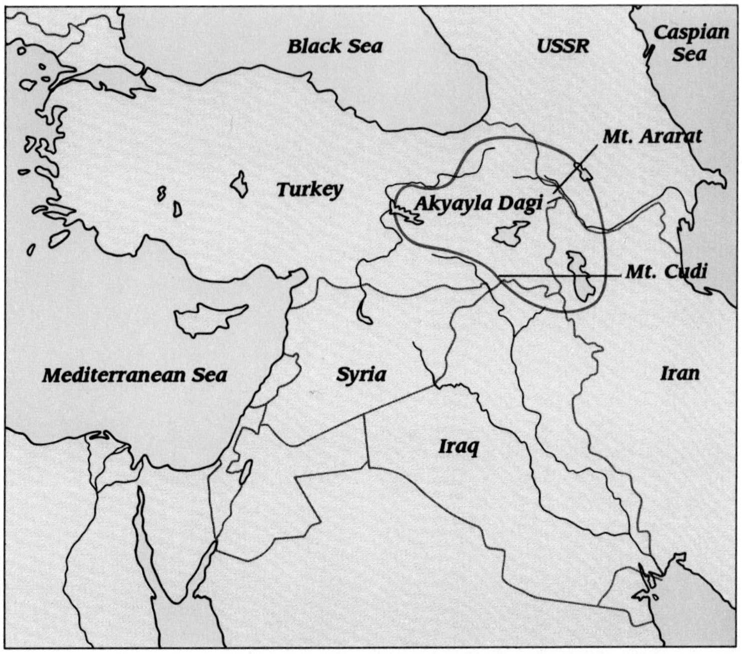

The ancient kingdom of Urartu, encircled on the modern-day map above, is prime hunting ground for Noah's Ark. The region is home to three sites—Mount Ararat, Mount Cudi, and Akyayla Dagi—that have particularly tantalized ark seekers.

view of biblical history. The words of the Bible are not distorted memories, they say, nor baseless fairy tales. Instead, Genesis's description of the Flood is an accurate report of a real historical event, one that is confirmed by the parallel legends of other cultures. The ark enthusiasts are unworried by the fact that scientists believe sea level on earth has not deviated by more than a hundred feet in the last 100,000 years, a change far less than that produced by the biblical Deluge, in which the ocean surface would have risen several miles. From their point of view, that discrepancy simply confirms that the great Flood was a miracle—by definition, an event that defies natural law. And the proof of that miracle, ark researchers believe, is perhaps as close as the peak on which the great ship came to ground.

The precise identity of that mountain has long been a matter of some dispute. Samaritan tradition places it in Sri Lanka, and Persian Jews once thought the ark landed on Iran's Mount Demavend. Some Muslims—who share many Old Testament beliefs with Jews and Christians—have pointed to the 'Aja mountain range in southern Saudi Arabia. And in the nineteenth century, a few scholars placed the ark in Afghanistan, in the mountains of the Hindu Kush.

Strictly speaking, such far-ranging locales are ruled out by the Bible, which places the ark's final resting place somewhere in "the mountains of Ararat." Yet that phrase itself covers considerable ground. The word *Ararat* is thought to be a variation of *Urartu,* the ancient term for the region that later became Armenia. During the ninth and eighth centuries BC, Urartu was a vast domain that encompassed parts of modern-day Turkey, Syria, Iran, Iraq, and Armenia.

Several possible ark sites fall within this large area, including the Turkish peak named Cudi Dag, or Mount Cudi. The name *Cudi* is a Turkish version of *Judi,* the name the Koran gives to the mountain on which Noah landed. The site of a mysterious stone structure known locally as the ship of Noah, Mount Cudi once housed several Christian monasteries—including the so-called Cloister of the Ark, destroyed by lightning in 766. Its later Muslim owners built a mosque at the same spot, dedicated to the memory of Noah's landing.

Most twentieth-century ark seekers, however, base their interpretation of the word *Ararat* on a secondary, and more restrictive, meaning that dates from the second century. By that time, Urartu had become Armenia, and the ancient term *Ararat* was applied only to one Armenian province, located in what is now eastern Turkey. In that relatively small area, the tallest mountain—a towering Turkish peak that overlooks the juncture of Turkey, Iran, and Soviet Armenia—is the one climbed by James Irwin.

Known to local residents as Agri Dagi, "the painful mountain," the peak is better known to Westerners as Mount Ararat, a name it acquired in recent centuries because of its popular association with the ark. Nearby villagers have no doubt that Noah's Ark came to rest on Ararat's lofty height. Local tradition identifies not only the graves of Noah and his wife and the plain where the animals were unloaded, but also the one-time site of the vineyard Noah is said by the Bible to have planted upon his arrival.

A slumbering volcano that occasionally stirs with earth tremors, Mount Ararat soars 14,000 feet from the surrounding plain to its spectacular peak, just under 17,000 feet above sea level. A massive icecap measuring twenty

A dark oblong shape near Mount Ararat's peak is visible at the center of this 1972 photograph, taken from an altitude of 450 miles by a NASA satellite. One ark enthusiast declared the shadow "about the right size and shape to be the ark," but NASA experts viewed only normal geologic features.

Rising majestically from a blanket of clouds, the ice-shrouded slopes of Mount Ararat loom above the plains of eastern Turkey. According to one religious tradition, it is not the mountain's daunting conditions that protect Noah's Ark from discovery, but the power of God.

square miles covers its highest point, extending downward in several slowly moving glaciers. According to many ark seekers, Noah's ship probably came aground near the very top of the mountain, the first portion to emerge from the universal sea. In later ages, the flow of glacial ice gradually transported the ark's remains downhill, they theorize. Some believe the vessel came to rest on an alpine plane just below the domed peak; others, that the ship lodged on a rocky ledge about 13,500 feet above sea level at a point overlooking what later became Soviet Armenia.

Today, such theories remain at best unproven, since no conclusive evidence of the ark's existence at those or at any other sites has been found. But modern ark seekers offer several reasons why even a large wooden structure would be hard to find on the Turkish mountain. Much of the difficulty, they point out, derives from the extremely harsh weather on Mount Ararat. The mountain trails are all but impassable for much of the year, and climbers must frequently contend with hailstorms and lightning as well as with avalanches and earthquakes. Temperature variations may also complicate the quest for the ark; seekers think that it may only become visible during rare warm spells, when the ice that covers much of the upper mountain thaws sufficiently to expose portions of the wreckage.

As if to further complicate matters, international politics greatly increase the difficulty of planning any expedition. Because of its proximity to the Soviet and Iranian borders, Mount Ararat has frequently been classified as a military zone, prohibited to climbers for reasons of security. In the late 1980s and early 1990s, it reportedly served as a base for Kurdish insurgents.

According to an ancient belief still held by some Christians and Muslims, however, adverse conditions and volatile politics have little to do with the ark's mysterious inaccessibility. The wreckage of Noah's Ark, they feel, is protected by nothing less than a divine force that will keep the remains safely hidden until the end of time.

Yet every age has had its adventurers who sought the

ark. In the third century BC, a Babylonian priest named Berossus stated that in his time people visited the ark to recover fragments of its pitch—the tarry coating used to make the vessel watertight. This, Berossus recorded, was used as a charm against evil. Interest in ark pitch continued through the Middle Ages, when it was thought that the substance, when dissolved in liquid, could serve as an antidote against deadly poisons. By that time, however, the ark was increasingly regarded as a holy relic worthy of a pilgrimage for its own sake.

One of the earliest accounts of a quest for the ark was recorded by the Greek author Faustus of Byzantium, a fourth-century chronicler of Armenia, in his *Historical Library.* Although Faustus couched his tale in quasi-legendary terms, his protagonist, Saint Jacob of Nisibis, was an actual historical figure of Faustus's own day who played a key role at the Council of Nicaea in 325. According to Faustus, Jacob decided one year to seek out Noah's Ark on a mountain—although modern-day readers disagree just which mountain is meant. Most ark seekers identify it with the modern Mount Ararat, a claim supported by some local traditions linked to Jacob's climb; scholars of ancient texts believe a more plausible interpretation of the text places the intended peak in the Gordian mountains, near Mount Cudi. Upon his arrival there, according to Faustus, the saint "prayed God most fervently to allow him to see the Ark of deliverance built by Noah."

Jacob was, in the words of Faustus, "accustomed to obtain from God all that he asked of Him," and he started confidently up the mountain's steep slopes. During the climb, Jacob and his companions became thirsty, and Jacob prayed again, this time for water. In answer, God sent a spring that burst forth where Jacob laid his head. Sixteen centuries later, a water source identified as Jacob's well was still pointed out to foreign visitors on Mount Ararat.

But Jacob of Nisibis was not destined to complete his quest. As he and his comrades slept near the summit, Faustus recorded, an angel appeared to Jacob in a dream. "That which you find on your pallet is wood from the Ark," said the heavenly messenger. "There it is. I bring it to you: It comes from the Ark itself. From this moment on," the angel continued sternly, "you shall cease desiring to see the Ark, for such is the will of the Lord."

When Jacob awoke, according to Faustus, he discovered that the angel had not misled him. A fragment that "seemed to have been sliced from a great piece of wood with the blow of an axe" lay before him. Obedient to the prohibition against seeing the ark itself, Jacob returned in triumph to his monastery. There, Faustus wrote, the piece of wood was carefully preserved.

According to some reports, that fourth-century relic may have survived into the twentieth century, making it by far the oldest known sample of wood said to be from the ark. Exhibited to nineteenth-century European travelers at the monastery of Echmiadzin, located at the foot of Mount Ararat, the wood was described by one Western observer as a small, dark quadrangular piece carved on one side. According to an American journalist who claimed to have examined it in 1932, however, the relic consisted of petrified wood, which at some point had been formed into a cross twelve inches high.

In the centuries after Jacob's abortive journey, few travelers are known to have sought the ark, although many records casually refer to its continued survival somewhere in Armenia. In a typical allusion, no less an authority than the thirteenth-century Italian adventurer Marco Polo confirmed the ark's general location. "You must know," he wrote, "that it is in this country of Armenia that the Ark of Noah exists on the top of a certain great mountain."

The next record of an expedition up Ararat dates from the mid-seventeenth century, in the form of an extraordinary—and probably highly embroidered—tale recounted by Jans Janszoon Struys, a Dutch traveler who had made a tour of Europe and the Orient. Struys was a somewhat luckless adventurer; at one point during his travels, he was captured and sold into slavery. Thus it was, as Struys told the story, that in June 1670 he and his new master were traveling near Mount Ararat when a pair of Carmelite monks approached them with an unexpected proposition. Somehow the monks had formed the notion that Struys was a talented surgeon. There was a hermit living high atop the mountain who was suffering from a hernia, they said. If Struys would agree to operate, they would reward his master with a large sum of money. According to Struys's account, the hermitage could be reached only after seven days of hard climbing. Strangely, after he and his companions had passed through a "dark and thick" cloud bank, two additional layers of "ice-laden" clouds, and freezing winds, the conditions seemed to grow more temperate.

At last they reached the hermit's cell, where an examination of the ailing monk revealed the hernial swelling. Although Struys possessed little medical experience, he so greatly feared the wrath of his master that he proceeded with a makeshift operation. Evidently, his efforts met with some success, ensuring a payment to Struys's owner. As for the Dutchman himself, he wrote that "the brave hermit thanked me so profusely that I was embarrassed. He added that his sacred vow prevented him from giving me rich presents, and that he had nothing more precious than a cross attached to a little silver chain."

The monk's offering, however, was no ordinary crucifix. In his twenty-five years on Mount Ararat, the hermit explained, he had visited the remains of Noah's Ark many times. His cross, he said, had been fashioned from a sample of wood taken from one of the great ship's timbers. "He removed it from his neck and gave it to me," Struys recounted. "It consisted of a little fragment of reddish-brown wood, and with it he gave me a piece of rock on which the Ark came to rest."

Struys was so amazed that he asked the hermit for a written statement attesting to the provenance of the wooden fragment and rock. The hermit readily complied. "I myself entered that Ark," he wrote, according to Struys, "and with my own hands cut from the wood of one of its compartments the fragment from which that cross is made."

With that document and his extraordinary prize tucked among his belongings, Struys made his descent through conditions so treacherous that he feared for his life at every turn. Although he arrived safely, and was later restored to freedom by a Polish ambassador, the experience left him badly shaken. "Neither the Ark nor the rock which cradles it," he insisted, "would have an attraction sufficient to draw me there again."

Today, no one knows what became of the fragment of stone, the hermit's written testimonial, or the mysterious wooden cross—although the description of the cross is certainly reminiscent of the relic at Echmiadzin. And Struys's account of his tortuous climb did little to inspire other adventurers. Indeed, it was not until the early nineteenth century that Mount Ararat drew explorers in significant numbers, among them a German academic named J. J. Friedrich W. Parrot, who undertook his quest in 1829.

A professor of natural philosophy from the University of Dorpat in Estonia, which was then a part of imperial Russia, Parrot was inspired to scale the mountain by a visit he had made to the Echmiadzin monastery. There an abbot showed him a small religious icon said to have been fashioned from the ark; history does not record if this was either the same relic recovered by Struys or the one attributed to Jacob of Nisibis.

Parrot was intrigued by the abbot's story, and by the tales of the Russian and Armenian climbers who joined him for his expedition. "They are all firmly persuaded that the Ark remains to this day on the top of Mount Ararat," he noted in his journals, "and that in order to ensure its preservation no human being is allowed to approach it."

Initially, Mount Ararat did seem to repel the approaches of Parrot and his party. On his first two attempts, the professor failed to reach the summit and sustained painful injuries. Undaunted, Parrot launched a third assault in October 1829. "Boldly onwards! resounded in my bosom," he later dramatically recounted. "We passed without stopping over a couple of hills; there we felt the mountain wind; I

Coffinlike Crate That Cradled Life

Through the ages, artists often have depicted Noah's Ark as a most unshiplike affair, with flat rather than curved sides and a squared-off stem and stern. In many illustrations of the story, including those shown here, the ark more closely resembles a floating crate than a traditional seafaring vessel.

Such portrayals resulted not from artistic whim but from serious biblical scholarship. Whereas an ancient Sumerian story of a worldwide deluge describes the survivors riding out the turbulent tide in a *magurgur,* meaning "very great ship," Old Testament scholars have long maintained that Noah and his cargo escaped the Flood in an enormous floating casket. In the original Hebrew text of the Book of Genesis, the ark is called *teva,* which means "box," "chest," or "coffer."

Using these literal interpretations as their guide, many students of the Bible conceived a vision of a box-shaped ark. Sharing that opinion is one modern-day student of the Flood story, Henry M. Morris, former chairman of the Department of Civil Engineering at Virginia Polytechnic Institute. Morris, a creationist who brought his technical training to bear on the question of the ark's design, reported in a 1971 paper that the ark was "essentially a huge box."

According to Morris's calculations, the vessel's "relatively great length (six times its width)" and its cratelike construction afforded it the stability to weather even "the chaotic hydrodynamic phenomena of the Flood." The engineer concluded that "the Ark, as designed, was admirably suited for its purpose."

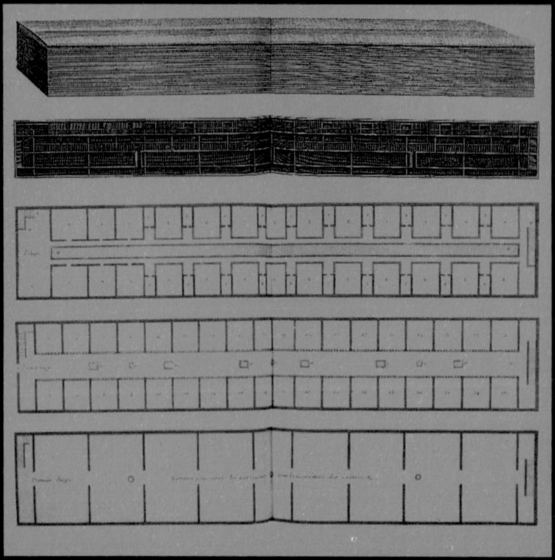

A 1722 book shows a monk's sketch of a long, narrow ark (top); his cross section and floor plans show three levels and many rooms.

Noah welcomes the returning dove to his squared-off ark, in this third- or fourth-century Christian painting from a Roman catacomb.

On this third-century coin, struck near Mount Ararat, Noah and his wife peer out from a boxlike ark. Also shown standing, they praise God.

In this painting from the 1400s, Noah, his family, and the animals emerge from an ark that resembles a house.

pressed forward round a projecting mound of snow, and behold! Before my eyes, now intoxicated with joy, lay the extreme cone, the highest pinnacle of Ararat."

Parrot laid no claim to having sighted Noah's Ark while on his climb, but even his declaration that he had reached the summit immediately became a subject of doubt and debate. At the time few experts believed that Mount Ararat's icy peak could ever be scaled. Parrot's ascent would not be verified by subsequent climbers until some years after his death. If he was in any way troubled by the challenges to his claims, however, he gave no sign. He had not ascended the mountain for personal glory, nor had he truly expected to discover the remains of Noah's Ark. His goal had been simply to stand on the ground where, he believed, the celebrated ship first came to rest.

Even so, Parrot's experiences enabled him to speak authoritatively on the likelihood of the ark's survival. "Should anyone now inquire respecting the possibility of remains of the Ark still existing on Ararat," he later wrote, "it may be replied that there is nothing in that possibility incompatible with the laws of nature, if it only be assumed that immediately after the Flood the summit of that mountain began to be covered with perpetual ice and snow, an assumption which cannot reasonably be objected to. And when it is considered that on great mountains accumulated coverings of ice and snow exceeding 100 feet in thickness are by no means unusual, it is obvious that on the top of Ararat there may be easily a sufficient depth of ice to cover the Ark, which was only thirty ells high."

By Parrot's day, however, the intellectual climate was becoming inhospitable to biblical wonders because of a widespread acceptance of revolutionary scientific beliefs. The new sciences of geology and paleontology, as well as the theory of evolution set forth in Charles Darwin's *On the Origin of Species by Means of Natural Selection* in 1859, seemed very much at odds with the teachings of the Bible, especially with those Old Testament passages that describe the creation and early history of the earth. In the Darwinist clubs that sprang up across Darwin's native land of England, the very idea that Noah's Ark had ever existed, much less that its remains had survived for centuries, began to seem quaint and outmoded.

Ironically, the new skepticism may have led to the deliberate suppression of one of the most remarkable ark sightings, at least according to some historians of the Ararat quest. Sometime in the mid-1850s, as the story goes, three unnamed British scientists determined to scale Mount Ararat in search of Noah's Ark, as others had done before them. In contrast to those earlier adventurers, however, the three men had apparently resolved in advance that their expedition would fail. If a thorough investigation did not produce any evidence of the ark, they supposedly

Known as the Ship of the Prophet Noah, this stone structure rests atop Mount Cudi, in eastern Turkey. Nearby residents, who claim to be Noah's descendants, conduct annual religious services at the site to commemorate the ark's landing.

Two Arab workmen pause before a layer of solidified river mud uncovered during Leonard Wooley's 1929 excavation at Ur. Wooley attributed the stratum of silt to "the Flood on which is based the story of Noah." Although similar deposits found in the region seemed to support his thesis, further analysis concluded that they were not all the result of a single deluge.

reasoned, then the veracity of the biblical tale of Noah would be disproved once and for all, clearing the way for more modern scientific beliefs. With this goal in mind, the three men hired an Armenian guide and his son, a boy named Yearam, to conduct them on their journey.

What occurred on that expedition is said to have remained a secret for almost sixty-five years, during which period Yearam emigrated to the United States. Not until 1915, when the aged Yearam fell ill, did the true circumstances of the trip begin to emerge. As he rested in bed at the home of Harold and Ida Williams, Yearam told a remarkable tale, which his American hosts carefully recorded in a notebook. He and his father, Yearam said, had been able to guide the trio of Englishmen up the mountain and to locate the ark with little difficulty, aided by a recent warm spell that had led to considerable thawing of the icecap. The vessel's remains, he claimed, were protruding from the side of a dripping glacier, allowing the British scientists to make a close examination.

Naturally enough, Yearam had expected the explorers to be excited by the find. Instead, he related, they were furious. The discovery of the ark, if it became known, would disprove their widely publicized beliefs and expose them to ridicule. Turning on Yearam and his father, the Englishmen supposedly extracted sworn oaths—under threat of death—that the Armenians would never reveal what they had seen.

For decades, Yearam said, he had kept the vow of silence, but with death close at hand, he had decided to let the truth be known. Yearam did die in 1920, five years after relating his dramatic account. But the matter did not end there. Two years before Yearam's death, according to Harold Williams, a strange item appeared in several newspapers, including one published in Williams's hometown of Brockton, Massachusetts. The papers supposedly said that one of the three British scientists who had originally commissioned the expedition now found himself suffering an attack of conscience over the incident.

The newspapers are said to have reported that the scientist, like Yearam, had made his own deathbed statement. He admitted that he and two partners had uncovered the remains of the ark and then cruelly terrified their Armenian guides into a lifetime of silence. Only now, facing his own imminent demise, did the nameless scientist feel he must reveal what he had seen on that distant Turkish peak.

By their own account, Williams and his wife treasured the clipping from the Brockton, Massachusetts, paper along with their record of Yearam's statement for many years, only to lose both in 1940 in a butane explosion at their private school in Louisiana. Ark researchers have since been unable to locate any newspaper articles about the British scientist's confession.

Today this convoluted tale must be treated with some skepticism, if only because no documentation has survived to confirm the story. At about the time that Yearam and the three anonymous scientists were said to have made their climb, moreover, Mount Ararat was subject to some highly systematic and well-documented expeditions. In 1850, a Russian colonel named Khodzko led a team of more than sixty people up the mountain as part of a long-term project to map the key terrain features of Transcaucasia. The expedition was a success, but Khodzko saw no evidence of any ark. Six years later, a British army major named Robert Stu-

An Armenian archbishop at the Echmiadzin monastery, located at the base of Mount Ararat, displays a crucifix resting in a golden casket. "This," the holy man told a visiting American in 1932, "is the portion of Noah's Ark that was brought down from Ararat by St. Jacob."

art led his own party to the peak, where he declared, incorrectly, that in reaching the summit he had succeeded where all who preceded him had failed—with the possible exception of Noah himself.

For all of Stuart's posturing, he, like Colonel Khodzko, freely acknowledged he had seen no trace of the ancient ship. It would be another twenty years before the intrepid Englishman James Bryce made his visit to Ararat, where he became the first explorer of modern times to secure what has been called physical evidence of Noah's Ark.

Bryce, who subsequently became the British ambassador to the United States, was one of the more distinguished people ever to attempt the climb up Ararat's forbidding slopes. A diplomat, jurist, historian, and author, he had been vacationing in the region when he took a notion to scale the mountain, largely to satisfy his curiosity. Hastily assembling a small party of four Kurds and seven Cossacks, Bryce and a companion began their trek in September 1876.

From the outset, Bryce had difficulty. At the last moment his interpreter had fallen ill, leaving the Englishman unable to communicate with his guides. Yet the party made their way up the mountain with little trouble until they reached an altitude of approximately 12,000 feet, at which point it became clear that Bryce's companion and the guides would travel no further. Bryce was not to be deterred. "I buckled on my canvas gaiters," he later wrote, "thrust some crusts of bread, a lemon, a small flask of cold tea, four hard-boiled eggs, and a few meat lozenges into my pocket, bade goodbye to my friend and set off."

Thus, armed with little but his tea and a hardy determination, Bryce continued his climb. Three of the guides trailed along, perhaps, he later suggested, "simply curious to see what would happen." After several more hours of arduous climbing, during which one of the guides decided to turn back after all, Bryce's stubbornness was rewarded. "I saw at a height of over 13,000 feet, lying on the loose blocks, a piece of wood about four feet long and five inches thick, evidently cut by some tool, and so far above the limit of trees that it could by no possibility be a natural fragment of one. Darting on it with a glee that astonished the Cossack and the Kurd, I held it up to them, made them look at it, and repeated several times the word 'Noah.' The Cossack grinned," Bryce recalled in his memoir *Transcaucasia and Ararat,* "but he was such a cheery, genial fellow that I think he would have grinned whatever I had said, and I cannot be sure that he took my meaning, and recognized the wood as a fragment of the true Ark."

Despite his rather flippant recollections of the discovery, James Bryce apparently took his find seriously enough to chip off a small piece of the wood with an ax before continuing his climb. Soon he reached the summit, and as he gazed out over the magnificent vista that stretched before him, he found himself feeling strangely chastened. "How trivial history, and man the maker of history, seemed," he wrote. "This is the spot which he reveres as the supposed scene of his creation and his preservation from the destroying waters, a land where he has lived and labored and died ever since his records begin, and during ages from which no record is left. Dynasty after dynasty has reared its palaces, faith after faith its temples, upon this plain; cities have risen and fallen and risen again in the long struggle of civilization against the hordes of barbarism. But of all these works of human pomp and skill, not one can be discerned from this height. This landscape is now what it was before man crept forth on the earth."

That mountaintop insight into the impermanence of human works may have contributed to Bryce's obvious skepticism about the wood he had found. "I am, however, bound to admit that another explanation of the presence of this piece of timber on the rocks at this vast height did occur to me," he wrote in his book, without specifying the alternative theory. "But as no man is bound to discredit his own relic," he added, "I will not disturb my readers' minds, or yield to the rationalizing tendencies of the age, by suggesting it." The fragment itself was never scientifically examined; it returned with Bryce to England, but its present-day whereabouts are unknown.

A Flood Remembered around the World

Stories of cataclysmic floods and righteous people who survive them are found in the traditions of many lands. The Babylonian epic of Gilgamesh contains a flood story similar to the biblical account of Noah but preceding it; some versions of the tale date back to the seventeenth century BC. Ancient Persia had a traditional flood story, represented in the painting below. And the Egyptian *Book of the Dead* tells of the sun god Atum, who ordered the ocean waters to rise up and drown wicked humanity. Atum eventually rescues a chosen few people, picking them up in his "boat of millions of years."

It seems natural to find deluge stories among peoples whose lives depended on the yearly flooding of river valleys. But similar tales appear in the traditions of other cultures as well. The Aztecs recorded a flood as one of five global catastrophes, as shown in the stone relief *(inset)*. In India, a sixth-century-BC Sanskrit tale features a man who is warned by a fish about a coming flood. The man prepares a ship, and when the waters rise and destroy all other beings, the fish tows the man to safety on a mountaintop. And in a gruesome twist on tradition, an Icelandic legend describes the slaying of the giant Ymir, whose blood gushes forth and drowns all other giants except for one pair, who escape in a boat and live to begin a new race.

Some early researchers took such far-flung tales as proof that a worldwide flood had indeed occurred. More recent expert opinion has it that early Aryan invaders from the Middle East and later Christian missionaries may have sown the seeds that grew into richly embellished deluge stories, later to be discovered by folklorists.

This detail from an Aztec calendar stone depicts the end of a cosmic era, when the world was destroyed by flood.

In a fifteenth-century Persian miniature that is titled Uj Ibn Anuq Tries to Destroy the Ark, a fish-wielding giant appears ready to sever the sail on Noah's Ark, while the patriarch discourses on deck. Noah is revered by Muslims as a prophet, and this giant is his legendary enemy.

Just six years after Bryce's adventurous Ararat ramblings, several popular newspapers in Europe recorded a far more sensational discovery on the same mountain. According to an 1883 article in a British newspaper called the *Prophetic Messenger,* a Turkish news release asserted that remnants of Noah's Ark had been found sealed in a glacier on Mount Ararat. The news release itself—first mentioned a few months earlier in a Dutch newspaper—has never since been located.

As detailed in the *Messenger,* the discovery came in the wake of a violent earthquake, a well-documented disaster that shook the region in 1883. The news release stated that shortly after the quake a team of Turkish officials and an attaché from the British Embassy in Constantinople started up the mountain to assess the damage. Before they reached the summit, they came upon a huge wooden structure, painted brown, that closely matched the biblical description of the ark.

According to the newspaper account, the heavy timbers of the ship, some of which were broken, could be seen emerging from beneath a massive overhanging glacier. Some of the officials were said to have entered the great vessel, penetrating three large compartments before encountering a wall of solid ice that filled the remainder of the ship. Fearing that the overhanging glacier was about to collapse on top of them, they reluctantly withdrew.

The questionable antecedents of this story, which was never confirmed by the Turkish government, led to almost universal disbelief. Newspapers in Constantinople and Great Britain regarded the claims as a blatant hoax, while a reporter for the *New York Herald* could barely contain his sarcasm. Commenting on the craft's apparent durability compared with modern-day ships, the writer suggested that the ark might have a future in the United States military—at last, he wrote, the navy would possess "at least one ship that will not rot as soon as it leaves a navy yard."

And yet other, better-attested climbing parties continued to find wood on the mountain. In a Russian expedition in 1888, E. de Markoff, a young student at the Imperial University in Moscow and a member of the Russian Imperial Geographical Society, may have inadvertently destroyed some fragments. During the climb, de Markoff came down with altitude sickness—a sometimes deadly physical reaction to oxygen deficiency at high altitudes. Hoping to revive him, his guides began to prepare some tea. As a fire was lit to boil water, the young explorer noticed markings on some of the burning pieces of wood. Only later did it occur to ark seekers that de Markoff may have glimpsed evidence of Noah's Ark going up in flames.

Indeed, although a number of witnesses claim to have seen or handled fragments of the huge ship, in nearly every case the relics have come to an unfortunate end. Sometimes the adventurers themselves have fared no better, as in the case of the explorer John Joseph, sometimes known as the Prince—or Archdeacon—of Nouri, a region of southern India. Little is known of Nouri, as he was usually called. A world traveler fluent in several languages, he claimed to be a Nestorian archbishop, although he was unable to provide any proof of his position in the hierarchy of that Asian branch of Christianity.

By his own account, Nouri first came to Mount Ararat in 1887, hoping to locate the source of the Euphrates River, which flows from Turkey through Syria and into modern Iraq. Nouri's first attempts to scale the mountain failed, but his third try—or, by some accounts, his eighth—succeeded beyond all expectations. Although he had not been looking for it, Nouri reported that he had discovered the remains of a wooden ark, filled with snow and ice and wedged in among a cluster of boulders. According to Nouri's account, he was able to climb inside the vessel and take a set of measurements, figures which, he claimed, exactly coincided with the dimensions given in the Bible for Noah's Ark.

Inspired by the discovery, Nouri formed an audacious plan. Unlike any previous student of the ark, he hoped to carry the great ship, piece by piece, off the mountain during a proposed fourth expedition to Ararat. Parceled up for transport, the ark could then be shipped to the United States, where, according to the confident archdeacon, he

A Deluge Deciphered

Although the world has long possessed the biblical account of Noah and the Flood, it was not until 1872 that an earlier version of the story was recovered by thirty-two-year-old George Smith *(below).* Smith was responsible for translating and classifying cuneiform-inscribed clay tablets the British Museum had acquired some twenty years earlier from archaeological digs in what had been the ancient Mesopotamian city of Nineveh. Smith had been fascinated since boyhood with the writings, and, haunting the museum, he had taught himself to read the wedge-shaped characters. In 1859, the museum took him on as an assistant to the Assyriologist.

One day thirteen years later, Smith was amazed to read on a broken tablet *(below)* a fragment of poetry describing a boat landing on a mountain and the release of three birds over flood waters. He realized he had found an earlier version of the story of Noah's Ark. But the text was incomplete, and the missing shards were not in the museum.

Reporting his find to the Society of Biblical Archaeology, Smith generated such public excitement that a London newspaper put up the money to send him to Nineveh to locate the missing tablet. There, among the discards of earlier expeditions, he completed the text. The poem proved to be a seventh-century-BC Assyrian copy of the earlier epic of Gilgamesh. It was, at that time, the world's earliest known record of the story of the Deluge. George Smith, who twice returned to Nineveh to research other tablets, died there of a fever at the age of thirty-six.

would reassemble it for exhibition at the Chicago World's Fair. By some accounts, Nouri managed to win the enthusiastic backing of a group of investors, but his ambitious scheme was halted when Turkish authorities refused to sanction the endeavor.

A few years later, while he was on a trip to San Francisco, Nouri was robbed and badly beaten. Injuries that he sustained in the attack landed Nouri in a mental hospital. The ill-fated cleric lived on only a few more years in this diminished condition, and he died shortly after the turn of the century.

With the dawn of the twentieth century, new challenges faced explorers in their search for an ark on Mount Ararat. Changing politics in the region, including rising tensions between Turks and Armenians, made it difficult for foreigners even to gain permission to attempt the mountain. French climber Louis Seylaz, who reached the summit on August 12, 1910, described the political climate along the Turco-Persian border as approaching martial law. To further complicate matters, many of the Kurdish guides, whose experience was vital to any expedition, had grown jaded and often untrustworthy.

Local villagers, however, continued to wander freely over the mountain, according to at least one former resident's account. In 1970, publicity about the search for the ark inspired a seventy-year-old Armenian by the name of George Hagopian to break sixty-two years of silence with the story of his own boyhood pilgrimage to the holy ship. Like the former guide Yearam, Hagopian was living in the United States by the time he told his story; like Yearam, he claimed that those who live near Mount Ararat are quite familiar with the ark's remains. But whereas Yearam's story was said to have been transcribed by others in a notebook that was subsequently destroyed, George Hagopian's story was preserved on cassette

British jurist James Bryce suggested that a hand-carved piece of wood he recovered from Mount Ararat in 1876 was part of Noah's Ark, but modern-day scholars offer another explanation: Records show that earlier pilgrims and explorers left behind on the mountainside crosses, containers, and other wooden objects.

tape. Subsequent stress analyses of his tape-recorded voice have shown that Hagopian, who died in 1972, genuinely believed what he said.

In his taped account, Hagopian recalled being taken to see the ark in 1908 by his uncle, who carried the boy on his shoulders up Ararat's steep slope. After a long climb, they saw a ship, partly covered in ice and snow and perched on a rock ledge over a high cliff. His uncle urged the boy to climb up on the structure. "The animals and people are not here now," he told his nephew reassuringly. "They have all gone away." Filled with awe, Hagopian scrambled onto the roof of the ark and bent to kiss it. But when he returned home, the other village boys calmly matched his story. "Yes," they said. "We saw that ark too."

Although the voice analyses verify Hagopian's honesty, his story has been called into question by those skeptical of the ark's survival. Hagopian, some suggest, may actually have visited a rare rock formation. "Significantly, the old man described the ark as one solid petrified mass, without nails or joints, covered with moss," freelance author and ex-fundamentalist Robert Moore pointed out in a 1979 article—a description that to Moore suggested a natural, rather than constructed, object.

In the decades following Hagopian's memorable experience, foreign explorers barred from easy access over land found that the advent of aviation opened up exciting new possibilities for explorations by air. Perhaps the most famous—but also the most implausible—aerial ark sightings were those described in the March 1939 issue of California's *New Eden* magazine by a Russian pilot named Vladimir Roskovitsky, who allegedly photographed the ark from the air during World War I.

In the years since the magazine article appeared, however, all but the most die-hard ark researchers have come to view it as a hoax, intended to raise money for a planned ark expedition. Their chief reason for skepticism is that Roskovitsky, said to have been a lieutenant of the Russian Imperial Air Service, cannot be shown ever to have existed. No documents for a pilot by that name have been found in Russian military records, nor does any Russian veteran who served near Mount Ararat during World War I recall a Lieutenant Roskovitsky. Those who believe the story, however, have an explanation for the author's use of a false name. By the time the article was published, they point out, the Russian pilot would have been a refugee from the

Tales of Noah's Living Cargo

The brief biblical account of Noah and his narrow escape from the Flood leaves much to the imagination. Naturally, the world's folk traditions have embellished the story with wondrous details of Noah and his passengers.

According to one tale, as Noah began gathering animals into the ark—depicted in the Romanesque mosaic below—he tried to leave the buzzing flies behind. But the devil appeared and said, "Either the flies go on board, or I do." Noah, choosing the lesser evil, shooed the flies inside. The devil stuck to that bargain, but he devised other trickery to get himself on board the ark, there to wreak havoc, as Finnish and Irish yarns relate, by creating the voracious mouse.

It was that mischievous mouse, say some European and Middle Eastern tales, that gnawed a hole in the ark's bottom, causing it to spring a leak. The dog rushed to the rescue, trying to plug the hole with its nose; this is said to be why dogs' noses are wet and cold. But the nose was not a good fit, so the snake helpfully stuck its tail in the hole, and there it stayed until the voyage ended. Meanwhile, the magpies allegedly refused to ride inside the ark but sat on the roof jabbering about the sorry state of the submerged world. Thus magpies came to be feared as omens of bad luck.

The mouse was not the only creature who sprang to being on the ark. According to Israeli myth, both the pig and the cat were created by God during the voyage to serve special purposes. Refuse was mounting in the close quarters of the vessel, so the resourceful Noah ran his hand down the elephant's back, and a pig sprang forth and happily set about eating up the ark's garbage. Similarly, the first cat was brought forth from the lion's back, to contend with rodents busily multiplying in the ship's stores of grain.

Other folk tales explain why two legendary animals are not seen today. The griffin, a proud creature with the body of a lion and wings of an eagle, haughtily refused to board the ark and was lost in the Flood. The unicorn entered the ark but was rudely thrown overboard in an argument.

After five months on the raging universal sea, when Noah dared to hope the waters were receding, he sent forth a raven—which was at that time a white bird—to look for land. It never returned but instead settled down to feed on a floating corpse. From then on, it is said, the raven's feathers have been black. Noah next released a dove, which returned bearing an olive branch—a sign of life—and God rewarded it with shining white plumage that never molts. The Bible records that when the dove was released again and did not return, God set a rainbow in the sky. According to one tradition in the southern United States, all the other birds flew through the rainbow, and that is how they got their colorful plumage.

Soviet Union. Fearing the long arm of Stalinist security forces, they say, he may well have written under a pseudonym to protect himself.

Whatever the truth of the story, the *New Eden* article was highly influential in inspiring later ark seekers, in part because its account of the ark is so detailed. The story begins by explaining that Roskovitsky was assigned to conduct high-altitude tests near Ararat during a mission to monitor Turkish troop movements. Equipped with oxygen tanks, he and his copilot had made two circuits high above the mountain when their attention was drawn to a half-frozen glacial lake. As they flew in closer, Roskovitsky's copilot pointed to something large and dark. Circling the mysterious object, the lieutenant thought it appeared to be the half-submerged hull of a huge ship.

At first, Roskovitsky assumed he had spotted some sort of German submarine, although he soon realized the impracticality of launching a submarine from a glacial pool halfway up a mountain. A closer look revealed two stubby masts and a flat catwalk running along the top of the vessel. Clearly, this was no submarine.

"We flew down as close as safety permitted and took several circles around," wrote the article's mysterious author. "We were surprised when we got close to it at the immense size of the thing, for it was as long as a city block, and would compare very favorably in size to the modern battleships of today."

Returning to his air base about twenty-five miles to the northeast of the mountain, Roskovitsky reported the find to his commanding officer. The captain was understandably intrigued, according to the ex-pilot's story, and he accompanied Roskovitsky on a second flight over the site. After seeing the remains with his own eyes, the base commander is said to have felt no doubt: The Russian Imperial Air Force had found Noah's Ark.

Excitedly, the commanding officer sent a report directly to his superiors in the city of Saint Petersburg, supposedly capturing the interest of Czar Nicholas II himself. Orders were issued to send two companies of engineers—a total of 150 men—to conduct a full-scale assault on Mount Ararat.

Within a month, the *New Eden* article continues, the ground force located the ark. Their findings, as passed on by Roskovitsky, included intriguing and previously unreported detail about the ancient wreck. "The Ark was found to contain hundreds of small rooms, and some rooms that were very large, with high ceilings," he wrote. "The unusually large rooms had a fence of great timbers across them, some of which were two feet thick, as if designed to hold beasts ten times the size of elephants. Other rooms were also lined with tiers of cages, somewhat like what one sees today at a poultry show, only instead of chicken wire, they had rows of small iron bars along the front.

"Everything was heavily painted with a waxlike paint resembling shellac, and the workmanship of the craft showed all the signs of a high type of civilization. The wood used throughout was oleander, which belongs to the cypress family and never rots; which of course, coupled with the fact of its being frozen most of the time, accounted for its perfect preservation."

Roskovitsky's account ends with the statement that the investigative officers sent a detailed report, with photographs of the ark, back to the capital of Saint Petersburg, directing it to the personal attention of Czar Nicholas. Unfortunately, the documents apparently met much the same fate as the soon-to-be-executed czar. The report was not simply lost in the tumult of revolution, the article asserts; instead, the material was said to have been diverted to none other than Leon Trotsky, the commissar of foreign affairs. The Bolshevik leader, perhaps fearing the counterrevolutionary impact of the discovery, may have destroyed the photographs or placed them in a permanently sealed file. Apparently Trotsky resolved to take no chances; the material was thought to be so explosive, according to the article, that even the special courier who had carried it to Russia was silenced by execution.

Even without the lost dossier, gossip current in the southern Russian army of that day does provide some confirmation of Roskovitsky's story. In 1945, almost thirty years after the alleged ark expedition, a Russian émigré and White Russian Army veteran by the name of Alexander Koor suggested that Roskovitsky may actually have been a first lieutenant named Zabolotsky, who, Koor reported, was widely rumored in army circles to have sighted Noah's Ark. Colonel Koor, who is said to have commanded Imperial Russian troops in the Ararat region during part of World War I, also recalled hearing about the subsequent ground expedition to the ark from a longtime family friend, army sergeant Boris V. Rujansky.

Although that anecdotal evidence may be heartening to those who believe the Roskovitsky account, critics point out what is apparently a fatal flaw: No matter who piloted them, Russian airplanes of that day probably could not fly as high as 13,500 feet, the altitude usually cited for the ark's remains. For the faithful few who still credit the story, Roskovitsky's vindication must await the increasingly unlikely day when the vanished report resurfaces. If that time ever arrives, they believe, the discoveries made by the czarist expedition could conceivably settle the matter of the ark's existence for all time.

In the turbulent years immediately following the Russian Revolution, expeditions to Mount Ararat were rare. It is hardly surprising, then, that one of the few ark sightings reported during that time—by J. Hardwicke Knight—appears to have occurred entirely by accident. Unlike Roskovitsky, Knight definitely existed. But he was a somewhat shadowy character. Although he claimed to be an archaeologist from New Zealand, Knight may also have been serving as an agent of the British government when he climbed Mount Ararat in August 1936.

Knight's own account of the experience is decidedly sketchy, apparently because he was on the run when he arrived in the neighborhood of Mount Ararat that summer—hoping to escape from what he called "embarrassing followers." Evidently his flight was unsuccessful; Knight was captured by a group of unidentified enemies who carried him off on horseback. Unable to communicate with his captors, Knight was taken to the mysterious kidnappers' headquarters and locked in a cellar to await his fate. After two days, he was released on foot without explanation. Taking his bearings, Knight realized that he was lost somewhere on Mount Ararat's frigid slopes.

Alone, Knight stumbled westward through a dense fog, hoping to reach safety. Dazed and weakened by his two days of captivity, he was thinking of little but survival when he came across a series of soggy timbers all but hidden in the ice and snow. At first, the weary traveler passed by without a second thought. Then, some buried instinct made him pause and turn back. "Anxious though I was to conserve my strength," he later recalled in correspondence with Eryl Cummings, an American ark researcher who participated in several expeditions to Ararat, "I was nonetheless curious, even if my curiosity had been slow to take.

"I satisfied myself that the soggy mass was indeed timber," he wrote. "Timbers extended in more than one direction; some were parallel and others perpendicular to them. The timbers could have been massive rectangular beams, although all I could see was the tops of them exposed level with the surface of the ground and it was not possible to tell how far they extended under the stones."

At first, Knight remembered, he believed he had discovered the remains of some sort of heavy wagon or barn. He broke off a piece of one of the beams, but, as darkness began to fall on the mountain, Knight admitted that he lacked the "composure which is necessary for a proper evaluation of an artifact."

Less concerned with archaeology than with his own survival, Knight left the site of the remains and pressed onward, eventually finding shelter in a small village at the foot of the mountain. Knight's wooden relic did not survive the journey, and it would be several more years before the thought even occurred to him that the timbers he had spotted might have been the remains of Noah's Ark. Once the idea took hold, however, Knight became convinced that his chance discovery had been enormously significant. As the

French amateur explorer Fernand Navarra climbs down into a deep glacial crevasse in 1955, on his third expedition to Mount Ararat in search of the ark. Just months earlier, Navarra's former climbing partner had abandoned the project, calling it "a vain enterprise."

years passed, he studied the accounts of others who had braved the mountain and realized that his findings were consistent with theirs. Knight was certain that he had located at least part of the ark.

In 1967, thirty-one years after his first superficial exploration, Knight returned to Mount Ararat and unsuccessfully attempted to relocate the site of his earlier adventure. "Perhaps some day archaeologists will devise some method of searching for and finding these evidences," wrote Knight. "Such researches must surely have the blessing of God. But for my own part, I am richly blessed to be one of the favored few who have been privileged to see and touch."

For some, however, the mere privilege of seeing and touching the elusive remains falls maddeningly short of the goal. Those caught up in the throes of "Ark Fever," as one author has called it, are longing to acquire positive evidence, tangible proof that will convince the world of the ark's survival. For George Jefferson Greene, an American mining engineer, this quest was to become an obsession. In the late summer of 1952, Greene was making a routine helicopter flight over Mount Ararat as part of a survey for his company. As his helicopter passed over the northeastern face of the mountain, according to his own account, Greene chanced to look down and spot an elongated object protruding from the ice.

Greene instantly concluded that he had seen the ark. Reaching for his camera, he told his pilot to maneuver the helicopter as close as possible to the object below. While the pilot edged closer and closer to the rocky surface of the mountain, Greene excitedly clicked away with his camera. As night began to fall, the two continued their impromptu photo session, with the pilot shifting the craft's course several times so that Greene could photograph the site from different angles. Greene later recalled that at one point their helicopter came within a hundred feet of the mountain's surface. Heedless of the danger, Greene kept shooting until he used up his film.

Back on the ground, the engineer developed the pictures and became more convinced than ever that he had located Noah's Ark. When blown up to large size, some of the exposures are said to have shown the vessel in great detail, even revealing what appeared to be laminated side panels. The photographs apparently also explained at least part of the difficulty that earlier mountain climbers had experienced in locating the vessel. The great ship was protected on one side by the wall of a high cliff; on the other by the mouth of a deep chasm. Moreover, it was embedded in a glacier, with only about a third of the ship's prow visible from the air.

Arming himself with a portfolio of convincing pictures, Greene tried repeatedly to interest various friends and associates in the prospect of launching an expedition to Mount Ararat. Now that he knew where the remains lay, he reasoned, it should be possible to actually climb in for a closer look at the ancient ark. In spite of what he considered the compelling evidence of the photographs, however, Greene's pleas for financial backing met with indifference. After years of fruitless effort, the frustrated engineer decided to strike out for British Guiana, where he found a job with a gold-mining operation.

On December 27, 1962, ten years after his fateful glimpse of the dark object, Greene was murdered by looters who ransacked his home. None of his possessions, including the photographs of the ark, were ever recovered. Ironically, it was only after Greene's murder that any interest began to surface in his now vanished photographs. A number of people, mainly those whom Greene had regarded as prospective backers, recalled having seen the photographs. One geologist was even able to make a sketch of one of them, showing a side view of the ark protruding from a wall of ice. But the disappearance of the original photographs meant final proof of the ark's existence was still lacking.

The intense, if belated, interest in George Greene's findings may have been inspired by the work of Fernand Navarra, one of the best-known ark researchers of the twentieth century. A wealthy French industrialist, Navarra put together several expeditions to Mount Ararat, beginning in 1952. In the course of these trips, he produced what is considered some of the most dramatic—and the most controversial—evidence of the existence of Noah's Ark that has ever been uncovered.

Navarra's interest in the ark took root at the age of four, shortly after he nearly drowned in a pond. To calm the frightened boy, Navarra's mother told him the story of Noah's Ark. Navarra never forgot the episode, and years later, when an Armenian friend told him tales concerning the survival of the ark, Navarra vowed to find it. A former army officer and experienced mountain climber, Navarra was well prepared for the rigors of Mount Ararat. Still, he could hardly have anticipated the stunning success of his very first expedition in August of 1952.

"The air was brilliantly clear," he later wrote. "An eagle wheeled in the sky. . . . In front of us was always the deep,

Eleven-year-old Raphael Navarra (above) waits as his father explores the crevasse where the boy has seen a dark shape; soon after, the climbing party hoisted a wooden beam to the surface (right). His son's find reminded Fernand Navarra of an Armenian saying: "To find the ark, one must be as pure as a child."

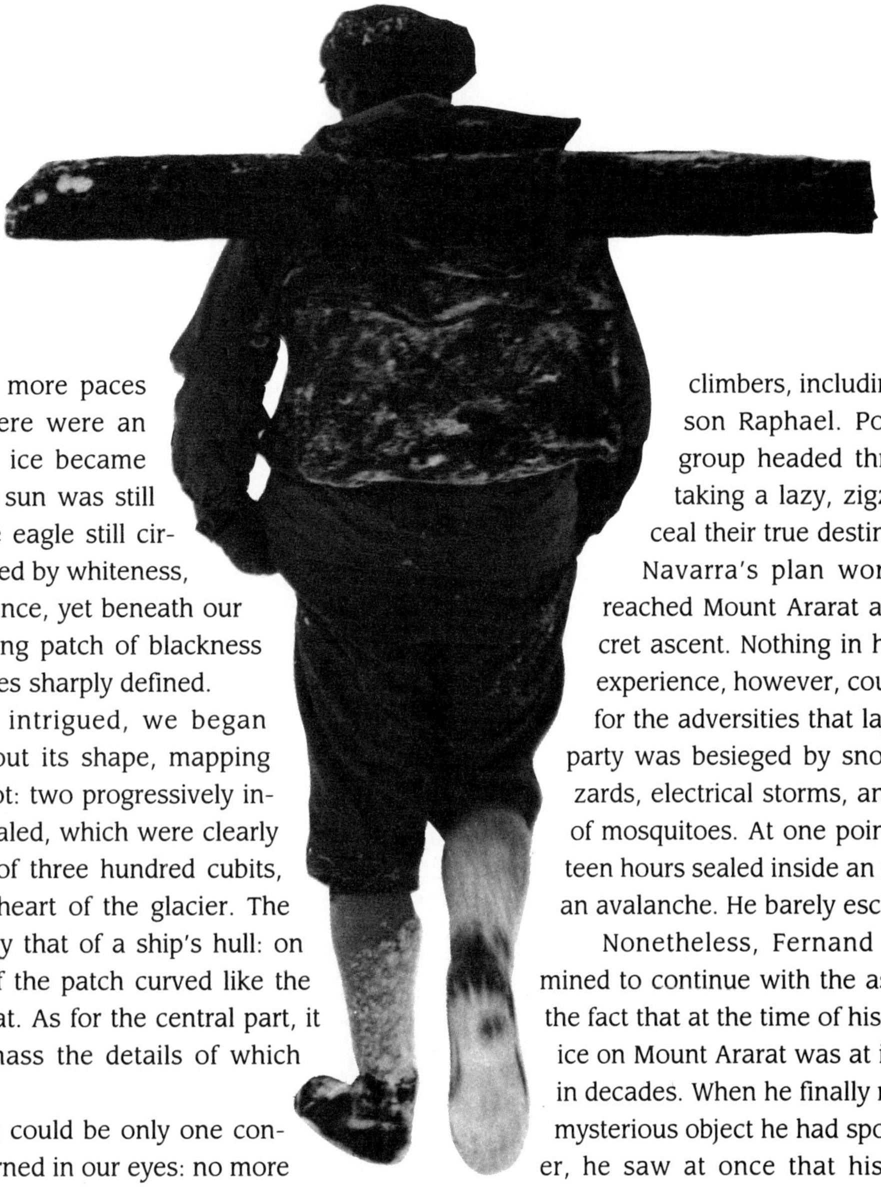

A triumphant Navarra heads down the mountain carrying the beam on his back, confident that he has found the ark. Controversy soon clouded his claim.

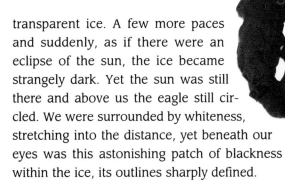

transparent ice. A few more paces and suddenly, as if there were an eclipse of the sun, the ice became strangely dark. Yet the sun was still there and above us the eagle still circled. We were surrounded by whiteness, stretching into the distance, yet beneath our eyes was this astonishing patch of blackness within the ice, its outlines sharply defined.

''Fascinated and intrigued, we began straightaway to trace out its shape, mapping out its limits foot by foot: two progressively incurving lines were revealed, which were clearly defined for a distance of three hundred cubits, before meeting in the heart of the glacier. The shape was unmistakably that of a ship's hull: on either side the edges of the patch curved like the gunwales of a great boat. As for the central part, it merged into a black mass the details of which were not discernible.''

For Navarra, there could be only one conclusion. ''Conviction burned in our eyes: no more than a few yards of ice separated us from the extraordinary discovery which the world no longer believed possible. *We had just found the Ark.*''

Despite his excitement, Navarra lacked the equipment to bore through the ice and investigate further. After taking a careful reading of his position, he was forced to withdraw from the mountain. ''We would indeed have given ten years of our lives to have had radar equipment that day,'' he ruefully commented.

After a brief and fruitless return to Ararat in 1953, which ended when he became ill, Navarra began preparing for a third campaign, the most ambitious yet. But his plans were hampered in 1955 when the Turkish government proclaimed the entire region off-limits to foreigners for reasons of national security. Undaunted, Navarra obtained travel papers for the rest of Turkey and set off with a group of climbers, including his eleven-year-old son Raphael. Posing as tourists, the group headed through Turkey by car, taking a lazy, zigzagging route to conceal their true destination.

Navarra's plan worked; his party soon reached Mount Ararat and launched their secret ascent. Nothing in his mountain-climbing experience, however, could have prepared him for the adversities that lay ahead. By turns, his party was besieged by snowslides, sudden blizzards, electrical storms, and even an infestation of mosquitoes. At one point, Navarra spent thirteen hours sealed inside an ice cave after dodging an avalanche. He barely escaped hypothermia.

Nonetheless, Fernand Navarra was determined to continue with the assault, encouraged by the fact that at the time of his furtive expedition the ice on Mount Ararat was at its deepest thaw point in decades. When he finally reached the site of the mysterious object he had spotted three years earlier, he saw at once that his struggles had been worthwhile. The ice mass had developed deep breaks and fissures, he later reported, plainly exposing pieces of the ark. But the fissures—some of which dropped as much as twenty-five to thirty feet down into the free-flowing water below—also represented a serious danger, Navarra's account continues. What had been a solid mass of ice during the previous expedition was now a perilous deathtrap, and it took the group of climbers two hours to traverse the final thirty yards to the vessel. How could he examine the ark without being swallowed up in one of the fissures? It was Navarra's young son who came up with the solution. Because he was small and light, he could be lowered into one of the large crevasses on the end of a rope.

There were several tense moments as Navarra waited while his son descended deeper and deeper into the pit of ice. Then, at last, the boy's excited cries floated up to his father: "There, I see it now! Yes, the boat is there, papa! I can see it as plain as day!"

Unable to restrain himself any longer, Navarra brought his son back up to the surface and climbed down into the crevasse himself, loosely secured by another rope. Soon the dark outline was within his reach; Navarra was on the brink of recovering the ark. Excitedly, he began brushing away the snow that covered the frozen shape. Instead of the hard wood he had expected, however, he discovered nothing but moraine, a gritty glacial debris.

In an instant, Navarra's joy vanished. "From a distance such a mistake was entirely possible," he later wrote. "The combination of dark lines really suggested the hull of a ship. But close by the illusion could no longer be sustained. I made every effort to deny the evidence. I went forward, brushing away the snow for another fifty meters. Everywhere the same! Nothing but dirt.

"I was horribly crushed. So, I had devoted eighteen years of my existence to a mirage! I had followed the tracks of the Ark historically and I had thought myself capable of recovering it geographically—after five thousand years. I had put together three expeditions, covered thousands of kilometers, risked the life of my son: all for a mirage."

Navarra would very likely have abandoned his quest then and there, but at that moment the voice of his son, echoing against the icy walls of the crevasse, reached him: "Papa, have you cut off a piece of the wood yet?"

"No," answered Navarra slowly. "It isn't wood. It's just some dirt from the moraine."

"Have you dug down?" asked his son.

In his disappointment, Navarra had not thought to do so. With renewed vigor, he began digging through the dirt and icy debris—and felt wood.

"There was a lump in my throat and I wanted to cry," he wrote. "I longed to remain there on my knees thanking God for having allowed me to succeed. After the most agonizing false start, I was experiencing the greatest joy of my life. I controlled my tears of happiness so as to be able to yell the news to Raphael: 'I've found wood!' "

With great effort, Navarra was able to cut off a five-foot section of a wooden beam he had uncovered. He found it to be of remarkable weight and obviously hand-tooled. Delighted by his find, Navarra now faced the problem of getting it safely past the Turkish officials who had denied him access to the mountain. Trusting to Providence, he sawed the timber into three sections and distributed them among the party's backpacks.

As expected, upon reaching the foot of the mountain, Navarra's party was stopped by Turkish soldiers who ordered them to empty their backpacks. But the soldiers paid little attention to the precious fragments. Later, Navarra speculated that they had dismissed them as firewood. Instead, the soldiers appeared intrigued by his camera equipment. Although cameras, like tourists, were forbidden on Mount Ararat at the time, the soldiers asked to have their pictures taken. Navarra cheerfully agreed, soon developing such cordial relations with the local officials that they offered permission to ascend the mountain, unaware of the unauthorized expedition he had just completed. Navarra politely declined.

Before returning to France, Navarra and his family traveled to Egypt, where he submitted a sample of his relics to the Archaeological Section of the Cairo Museum. According to one museum expert's visual inspection, the wood appeared to be roughly 5,000 years of age—a figure that seemed consistent with the implied biblical date of the Flood, about 2350 BC.

Later study in France and Spain also indicated that the wood was several thousand years old, a judgment based on its color, density, and degree of fossilization. But subsequent radiocarbon dating at the University of California, the National Physical Laboratory in Middlesex, England, and two private laboratories in the United States contradicted those findings. Radiocarbon dating, which measures the radioactive decay of carbon-14, a substance found in all living things, is one of the most widely accepted measures of the age of organic artifacts. Results from the tests suggested that Navarra's relics were only about twelve hundred years old, rather than several thousand. Undaunted, ark enthusiasts argued that radiocarbon-dating techniques might for some reason fail to produce accurate results in this extraordinary—and presumably miraculous—case.

In view of the conflicting findings, Navarra's evidence remains a source of debate between archaeologists and ark researchers. Some scientists have suggested an alternative source for the wood based on the carbon-14 results dating it to the eighth century. At that time, they theorize, local religious orders may have built wooden structures to house hermits or pilgrims visiting the holy mountain, much like the former monastery of Saint Jacob on Ararat's lower slope. Navarra, they propose, may have found the remnants of one of those wooden huts.

The possibility of human-made structures on Ararat could also explain why the various wooden specimens reported by Bryce, Knight, and Navarra differed so greatly. Bryce's sample had to be hacked off with an ax, Knight's wood was soft and easily broken by hand, and Navarra's was heavy and hand-tooled. Perhaps, speculate the scientists, each found part of a different structure or remnants of wooden crosses erected by previous climbers.

Navarra himself, however, harbored no doubts. "For me it is a certitude," he wrote in 1956. "I have found the Ark of Noah." To prove his point, Navarra returned several times to Mount Ararat, finding still more wood to buttress his claim. The results of tests conducted on the new wood were once again disappointing, however, suggesting that these samples dated from the seventh century.

As Fernand Navarra battled his critics, another equally tenacious ark hunter quietly continued his own quest for the ship, a search inspired and guided by what the seeker considered a divine vision. A stoutly religious Bulgarian, John Libi believed the location of the ark had been revealed to him in a dream. Between 1954 and 1969, Libi made a total of eight assaults on the mountain, enduring a series of hardships that would undoubtedly have discouraged a less dedicated seeker. At various times, Libi found himself buried in snow up to his neck, pelted by hail the size of tennis balls, and stalked by mountain lions. He also survived a thirty-foot drop onto a rocky ledge, lost his equipment in a torrential rainstorm, and braved an attack by bears—one of whom, Libi claimed, threw rocks at him. Sadly, Libi's extraordinary determination was not rewarded. When, at the age of seventy-three, he finally found the location he had seen in his vision, the ark was nowhere to be found.

In recent years, the claims of amateur explorers such as Libi and Navarra have drawn support from some unlikely quarters, including the United States Air Force. As early as 1960, when both men were midway through their respective explorations, American air force pilots stationed at Adana, Turkey, began reporting sightings of the ark. The pilots, who were attached to the 428th Tactical Flight Squadron, had been told of the relic by a Turkish liaison pilot who accompanied them on routine observation flights around Mount Ararat that afforded little more than a quick glimpse of the mountain. The flights passed uncomfortably close to the border of the Soviet Union, which had recently shot down an American plane in the area, and pilots were discouraged from lingering on their aerial rounds.

In the summer of 1960, Second Lieutenant Gregor Schwinghammer was making a counterclockwise pass around Ararat when he noticed what he later described as "an enormous boxcar or rectangular barge visible in a gully high on the mountain."

"We were coming down from 5,000 feet," the pilot told Charles Berlitz years later, during an interview conducted for Berlitz's 1987 book *The Lost Ship of Noah.* "I think we were at more like 3,000 feet when we sighted it. I remember that we were doing 380 knots. The Turkish liaison pilot said to us, 'That's where Noah's Ark is supposed to be. Look! You can see it now!' "

To Schwinghammer, it appeared that the ark was snagged on a protruding ledge, as if it had been sliding

Eerily boatlike in shape, what has come to be known as the Phantom Ark is outlined in rock on a slope sixteen miles southwest of Ararat. This first aerial photograph of the area, made in 1959 by Turkish military surveyors, drew worldwide attention to the enigmatic site.

down the mountainside. Unfortunately, fuel was running low in the aircraft. Concerns about this and about the proximity of Soviet air space made it impossible to slow down and take photographs of the site.

Nevertheless, the object on top of Mount Ararat remained a fixed image in the pilot's mind. "We used to talk about it in the bar after flying," he recalled. "Some of the pilots thought it was the ark and others didn't know what to think. I was not convinced about that but I knew that I had seen a large rectangular building like a barge or a ship high up on the mountain."

For two decades, Schwinghammer made no visual record of the sighting, but in 1983 he began to fear that he might one day forget the details of what he had seen. A friend with some artistic ability helped out by producing an image that Schwinghammer, by then a commercial airline pilot, felt was a good representation of the ark site. Soon afterward, perhaps as a result of publicity associated with his sighting, Schwinghammer is said to have received an unsolicited pamphlet on ark research that included a drawing of the lost ship. Startlingly similar to Schwinghammer's commissioned sketch, the picture in the pamphlet was based on the verbal description provided by George Hagopian of his 1908 trip to the ark.

Schwinghammer's impression was that the two sketches were virtually the same, showing a large rectangular shape banked on a ledge near a precipice. The only difference was that Hagopian had noticed windows along the top of the object, a detail Schwinghammer had not seen. Schwinghammer attributed this discrepancy to the fact that the windows appeared too small to have been seen from a fast-moving aircraft.

Nor was this the only apparent confirmation of Schwinghammer's story. Some of his fellow pilots, including Ben Bowthorp, who had been a first lieutenant at the time, also remembered glimpsing what they believed to be the ark. "On Ararat we saw something," Bowthorp said in a 1985 interview. "It was about two-thirds of the way up the mountain, made of wood, and it looked like a boat or a wooden boat-shaped wall. I don't know who first said it was Noah's Ark. We all discussed it. Most of us felt it could be, since that's where it's supposed to be."

For a minority of ark researchers, however, the question of whether the ark is "supposed to be" on Ararat itself or on another mountain remains wide open. In the 1980s, a former merchant marine officer named David Fasold antagonized many ark researchers with his claim that the seekers on Ararat are climbing up the wrong peak. The ark, he said, is snugly encased in a ship-shaped rock formation roughly sixteen miles southwest of Ararat, 6,350 feet above sea level on the so-called Akyayla Dagi, or High White Plain. Rather than packing food and equipment up a dangerous slope, would-be visitors can reach it in good weather by hiring a taxi in the nearby town of Doğubayazit, then hiking about half a mile to the site.

Although he became the most persistent advocate of the significance of the odd formation, which has come to be known as the Phantom Ark, David Fasold was not the first to spot it. Identified by some local residents as the ship of Malik Shah, an ancient ruler, the once obscure structure first drew world attention in 1959, when it was inadvertently photographed during a routine aerial land survey by the Turkish government.

As Captain Ilhan Durupinar, a photographic interpreter, examined the survey images in a three-dimensional projection, his attention was drawn to a smooth oval hill surrounded by a raised ridge reminiscent of the ribs of a boat. Given the proximity of Mount Ararat, the formation seemed worthy of further study. Government engineers sent to examine the site more closely measured the structure's length at approximately 500 feet, its greatest width at 150 feet, and the height of the surrounding ridge at 45 feet. Allowing for the possibility that overlying mud and rocks may have spread the ark from side to side over the centuries, the figures could be said to be in agreement with the biblical account of the proportions of Noah's Ark.

The next year, an international expedition that included officers of the Turkish army revisited the anomaly. After taking more measurements, the team came up with a drastic way to determine whether a ship lay under the rocks and mounded soil. Under the supervision of the Turkish soldiers, team members exploded dynamite against one portion of the hill. When no inner chamber or buried beams were found, interest in the Phantom Ark diminished. Scientists, journalists, and most other observers agreed with the conclusion that the formation was actually an unusual geologic uplift of mud and lava.

In 1977, an American anesthetist named Ronald Wyatt visited the Phantom Ark, having heard about the formation while in the Middle East on other business. Not far from the shiplike structure, he made a crucial find: a large stone with a single hole at one end that appeared to him to be an ancient anchor. In the years that followed, he would discover several more of the strange stones.

Wyatt made another trip to the site in 1979, but it was not until 1984 that the Phantom Ark returned to public attention. Accompanied by Wyatt, several prominent ark researchers visited the formation and gathered sacks of wood, soil, and stones, which they intended to subject to scientific examination in the United States.

On Akyayla Dagi, self-styled "ark-ologist" David Fasold points to the Phantom Ark rock formation, which he believes conceals Noah's Ark. A veteran marine salvager, Fasold asserts that, whether it lies underwater or underground, "I know a ship when I see one."

Alerted to the scheme, the Turkish government intercepted several of the sacks in Istanbul, claiming them as the national property of Turkey. Wyatt, however, had already returned to New York with other samples, which he displayed to the press. Tests of Wyatt's materials were not publicized (although they are said to have been shared with the Turkish Ministry of Culture), and for most observers the matter was once again closed. But by then the controversy had brought the rock formation to the attention of David Fasold, who now joined with Wyatt in studying the ark-size anomaly. Although the two differed in their religious beliefs—Wyatt was a fundamentalist Christian, Fasold more ecumenically inclined—both suspected the ark might be evidence of an earlier age, of an ancient civilization wiped out by a vast deluge.

Bringing his years of experience in ship salvage to bear on the intriguing problem, Fasold suggested to Wyatt that a sophisticated type of metal detector would allow them to examine the purported wreck without unearthing it. After acquiring the device, the two men set off for Doğubayazit, arriving in March 1985 to find the village covered with winter snow and the roads impassable by car. Stumbling through high drifts with the metal detector, Fasold and Wyatt reached the supposed ark site, which Fasold now beheld for the first time.

As they and their Turkish guides came within sight of the formation, "Christian and Muslim paused on that crest in reverence of what lay below them," Fasold recalled in 1988. "The sight before me awakened a faint recollection that suddenly rushed forward, the memory of a past event so terrifying and violent as to be unimaginable. It is an instinctive fear," he wrote, "that has been transmitted through inheritance from the survivors of the Deluge and can be awakened by the sight of the Ark.

"I descended the hill," David Fasold remembered, "as if in a dream, passing through the ages, and as a pilgrim, to the beginning of time." After shaking himself free of that uncharacteristic reverie, Fasold aided Wyatt in making some preliminary readings of the site. Almost immediately, the two discovered what they believed to be evidence of the very structure they were seeking. According to their reports, the scanner revealed traces of iron in long lines, which were intersected by other lines at fixed intervals. To Wyatt and Fasold, the interpretation was obvious: They had detected the nails embedded in the beams and giant cages of Noah's Ark.

The explorers then went on to trace out the boat in greater detail. Nine transverse lines, apparently nail studded, ran across the structure; thirteen other lines traced its apparent hull, curved rather than rectangular in shape, which pointed toward Mount Ararat. By now, Fasold had formed a theory to explain how the ark could have ended up at such a relatively low altitude. Originally, he said, it had beached high up in the region known as Akyayla Dagi, but an an-

Large, drilled stones like this one, says Fasold, were used as the ark's anchors. The explorer bases his belief on a quote from the Gilgamesh epic: "There was no crossing death's waters" without "the stone things." Experts counter that the stones appear—and are destroyed—in tablet X of the epic; the flood story takes place in tablet XI.

cient mud slide had carried it far downhill. The flow stopped only when the ark's remains struck a boulder, producing a still-visible dent in the structure's western wall.

As a shipping expert, Fasold considered the rounded form of the Phantom Ark far more plausible than the box shape insisted on by most ark seekers. But he remained puzzled about one key point: How could the individual ribs of the hull have been preserved so completely in the surrounding ridge? Surely a violent mud slide would have broken up any wooden ship.

Fasold's own answer—a controversial one that helped lead to a rift between him and Wyatt—was that the ark was not made of wood after all: Instead, like many ships built since the 1940s, the ark was constructed of lightweight concrete. Noah had built the great ship, Fasold asserted, by plastering a mixture of pumice, bitumen, natron, and other materials onto reeds woven over a framework of wooden beams. The biblical term *kaphar,* traditionally translated as "tar" or "pitch," actually referred to the reed "covering," according to Fasold's admittedly amateur linguistic research. Furthermore, the phrase *gopher wood*—a mysterious term that occurs nowhere else in the Bible—was the result of a copying error, Fasold said; what the original text probably referred to was *gophrîyth,* or brimstone, a reference to the concrete.

Whatever the merits of those biblical reinterpretations, Fasold and Wyatt's identification of the ark gained strong official support in June 1987 when the government of Turkey's Agri province declared the Phantom Ark site a state park. Marked by a sign reading Nu'hun Gemisi, Turkish for Noah's Ark, the formation became the center of a tourist facility, complete with a bus parking lot, a stainless-steel kitchen, and a meeting room capable of accommodating forty people.

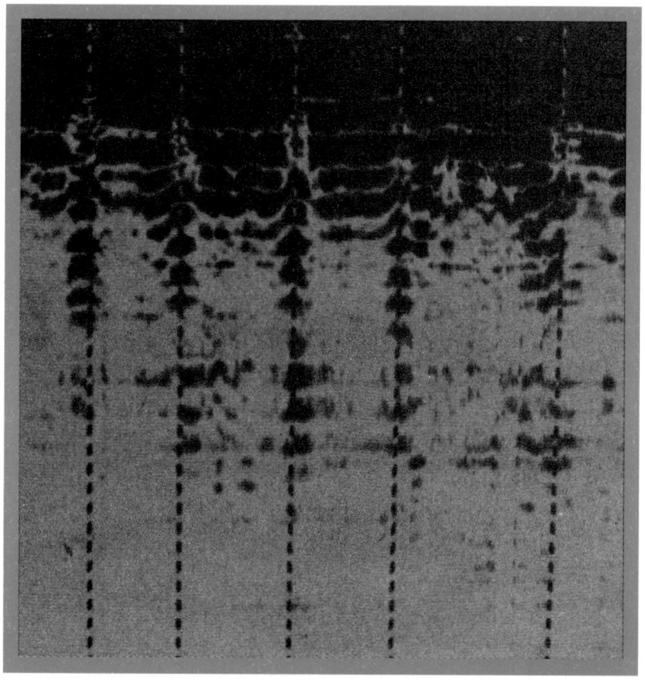

Fasold claims these ground-radar readings of the Phantom Ark reveal evenly spaced support posts, like those used in Sumerian ships. His findings are unconfirmed.

Later in the same summer, a research team headed by M. Salih Bayraktutan of nearby Atatürk University and John Baumgardner of Los Alamos National Laboratory, who had become interested in the site through David Fasold's researches, undertook an extensive geophysical study of the site. In a report published that November, Bayraktutan and Baumgardner appeared cautiously optimistic about prospects for finding the ark underground. Ground-penetrating radar, a high-precision magnetometer, and a small seismograph had revealed a number of interesting subterranean structures.

Among the more intriguing was a formation detected by both radar and seismograph: a reflective surface at a depth of twelve to twenty-four feet that could either be "the transition between the overlying clay soil and underlying bedrock or, alternatively, a material other than bedrock such as the petrified remains of a large boat." Although the report pointed out that "a large man-made structure in the site is an attractive way to account for the highly anomalous feature," the team concluded that only core drilling could determine whether the site was merely a geologic rarity or in fact the ark of Noah.

In line with that reasoning, the team returned the next summer to obtain a series of core samples from the site. The results were disappointing. Although team members differed on the interpretation of the drilling, Baumgardner himself had no doubts. Despite his interest in finding the ark, he believed that the samples demonstrated that the site was in all probability merely a ridge of basement rock. In his judgment, a mud slide flowing downhill had apparently gone over and around the unusually prominent rock, forming the almond shape of the Phantom Ark.

Although Fasold and others dispute that conclusion,

the majority of ark researchers, who still favor Mount Ararat, are also critical of the Phantom Ark. A literal reading of the Old Testament continues to suggest to them that Noah built a rectangular ship, not a tapered one, and the dimensions given in Genesis, in their view, specify a significantly smaller vessel. Fasold has also failed to convince more scientifically minded observers that iron nails, the cornerstone of his metal-detector evidence, could have been fashioned in 2350 BC, almost a thousand years before the metal was commonly used. (From his point of view, of course, the existence of iron nails before the Iron Age simply proves that earlier civilizations preceded the Deluge.) And neither historians nor pro-Ararat ark seekers can muster much enthusiasm for the theory that gopher wood was actually a form of concrete.

Controversy has also enveloped Ron Wyatt's anchor stones, which turned up in increasing numbers during the 1980s, almost always near the sites of ancient graves. According to Wyatt and Fasold, the stones acted as drogues to steady the ark during the violent phases of the Deluge; as they struck against the mountainside, the ropes holding them broke off, depositing the stones over several miles. Skeptics have suggested that the stones are simply burial markers. The holes, they claim, were drilled so that the tombstones could be dragged to the graveyards by rope.

For all their criticism of the Phantom Ark, however, the Ararat supporters have ultimately fared little better than Fasold in proving their case. Despite many intriguing anecdotes, despite all the expeditions and reported sightings, there is still no conclusive evidence that the ark actually exists on Ararat—no generally accepted sample of sufficiently ancient wood, no definitive photograph. Those who quest for the ark on Mount Ararat are left only with the accumulated body of sometimes contradictory sightings, the earliest of which are thought by many scholars to apply to other mountains.

Yet for those convinced the ark lies on Ararat, the tantalizing evidence acquired so far offers reason enough to continue exploring that perilous mountain. For former astronaut James Irwin in particular, the quest became its own reward. "We didn't find a shred of evidence of the ark, not a trace," he wrote of the 1982 climb in his book *More than an Ark on Ararat.* "So what was the trip all about?" For him, he continued, the benefit was an "inward spiritual journey, which is the most splendid adventure of all."

In the 1980s and 1990s, several more ascents of Mount Ararat were planned, many of them designed to make use of the latest mountain-climbing technology. But Irwin's repeated expeditions were among the few to succeed in reaching the site; other groups, lacking a well-known public figure like Irwin to attract support, were thwarted by insufficient funds and by difficulty in obtaining permits. Meanwhile, the familiar problems of an inhospitable climate and political instability remained the most significant obstacles to would-be adventurers. In 1985, four different teams of climbers reported they had been chased off the mountain by local dissidents brandishing the latest Soviet weaponry.

If, someday, explorers find an ancient ship stranded on that remote mountainside, will it mean that a seemingly legendary part of the Bible has, in effect, been proven to be sober fact? Most ark researchers accept that for some, no evidence, no matter how compelling, will ever be enough. Colonel Irwin, who risked his life searching for Noah's Ark, remained philosophical on the question. "There will always be skeptics," he told a reporter in 1984. "There are people who don't believe we walked on the moon."

Not far from the site of the Phantom Ark, Fasold found this engraved stone, perhaps one more clue to the ark's whereabouts. He translates the Armenian inscription thus: THIS IS • ARK MINE • RESURRECTION • SON OF GOD • THE BOAT • OCTOBER 1245.

Psychics Who Seek the Past

"Assume parapsychology exists and use it as a tool,'' advises Stephan Schwartz, a pioneer in the field of archaeology—psychic archaeology, that is. Schwartz, who has dispensed paranormal advice at a number of excavations around the world, believes that the hidden potential of the human mind is a valuable instrument, one that may soon take its place alongside the archaeologist's trademark pickax and shovel. And it appears that some scientists agree with Schwartz: Over the course of the twentieth century, a growing number of archaeologists have put aside their characteristic skepticism and called on psychics to help uncover secrets locked deep within the earth.

Simply put, the goal of the archaeologist is to find hidden objects, a task for which psychics seem ideally suited. Seers who claim to view the world as it appeared centuries ago or who demonstrate an uncanny ability to visualize buried artifacts add a powerful new dimension to the search for ancient cultures. For investigators of paranormal phenomena, archaeology offers an exciting demonstration of the potential of psychic ability—and, possibly, a foolproof test of its existence. ''It's a very clean experiment when a psychic tells you first to go to a place, then tells you what you will find there,'' observes parapsychologist Schwartz. ''The stuff is either there or it isn't. It cuts through all the smoke screen about magic tricks and fraud.'' Four experiments in psychic archaeology—independently conducted by Schwartz and three archaeologists at digs around the globe—are detailed on the following pages.

Clarence Weiant at Tres Zapotes

An Old Man's Vision Saves a Mexican Dig

For four months in 1939, archaeologist Clarence Weiant endured torrential rain, hip-deep mud, and tarantulas as he toiled at a site near the Mexican village of Tres Zapotes, about 100 miles southeast of Veracruz. Previously, the area had yielded evidence of the intermingling of three ancient cultures—Aztec, Mayan, and Olmec—but as the end of the digging season approached, Weiant was empty-handed.

The problem lay in knowing where to look. Fifty mounds, once the sites of temples or monuments, dotted a two-mile-long stretch of land. While each held the promise of buried artifacts, Weiant and his crew focused on one seemingly likely mound. They dug cautiously to avoid damaging a potential find, often using their bare hands.

"Hardly anything turned up," Weiant later recalled. "It was pretty discouraging after all that work." Then one evening Emilio Tegoma, an elderly member of the crew, approached him. "The old man saw that I was disappointed," Weiant recounted. "He came up to me and said that tomorrow, if I would shift the digging to where he told me, I would have results."

Weiant had studied parapsychology but was reluctant to stake his entire excavation on what might be only a hunch. However, the old man had confidence in his ability to see hidden objects. Leading Weiant to a cluster of four low mounds, Tegoma insisted that they would find buried treasures there.

The new location was well isolated from the sites of previous discoveries. Nevertheless, facing the dismal prospect of a barren season, Weiant took a chance; his crew commenced digging. "Within twenty minutes of the first shovelful, I knew the choice was the correct one," he said later.

In time, the mounds yielded scores of artifacts, many of them more than 2,000 years old, that proved earlier theories about the region. But for many years, Weiant remained silent regarding Emilio Tegoma's psychic insights, convinced that "no one would pay any attention to parapsychology combined with archaeology."

For weeks Emilio Tegoma, a Mexican peasant in his eighties, worked quietly alongside Clarence Weiant and his crew at the Tres Zapotes excavation before revealing his unusual talent for sensing hidden objects. Only when the archaeologist's determination seemed to flag did Tegoma step forward, using his psychic ability to guide Weiant to a cache of buried artifacts.

Workers cut an exploratory trench across an earthen mound selected by seer Emilio Tegoma. Despite archaeologist Weiant's hesitation, the site produced most of the excavation's treasures.

This unusual laughing figurine, discovered within the first twenty minutes at the site suggested by Emilio Tegoma, immediately validated the elderly man's psychic insight.

A pair of mysterious stone yokes, carved to resemble the head of a frog and the mouth of a jaguar, were among the relics that were found with Emilio Tegoma's help. Scholars speculate that the yokes were once placed around the necks of human sacrifices, holding them fast as priests tore the hearts from their chests.

Professor J. Norman Emerson

A Psychic Informant on the Iroquois Trail

In a March 1973 address to a gathering of Canada's foremost archaeologists, J. Norman Emerson created a sensation by expressing his unqualified belief in what he called "intuitive archaeology." A respected professor of anthropology at the University of Toronto and founder of the Ontario Archaeological Society, Emerson declared, "It is my conviction that I have received knowledge about archaeological artifacts and archaeological sites from a psychic informant who relates this information to me without any evidence of the conscious use of reasoning."

Professor Emerson's "psychic informant" was actually close friend and fishing companion George McMullen. Some months earlier, McMullen had used his alleged psychic ability to successfully diagnose a baffling medical problem of Emerson's, and he subsequently provided valuable guidance at a troublesome excavation. Thus, in May 1973, when one of the professor's former students, C. S. Reid, was perplexed by evidence uncovered on a dig just east of Toronto, Emerson again requested McMullen's services.

As soon as Emerson and McMullen arrived at the site, the seer immediately began striding across the ground, spilling out to archaeologist Reid his impressions of ancient structures and their uses. After two years of digging, Reid had located signs of a 1,000-year-old Iroquois long house, a large communal home fashioned of bent saplings covered with bark. But he had only partially traced the outline of the protective wooden fence, or palisade, that traditionally encircled Ontario Indian villages. Within minutes, McMullen successfully completed the palisade's outline. More important, over the next week, he pinpointed the site of a second long house and correctly identified its purpose.

For Professor Emerson, McMullen's achievements confirmed his own conviction that psychic ability could play a key role in the future of archaeology. Proclaimed the archaeologist, "A whole new vista of man and his past stands ready to be grasped."

Though he describes himself as an "average guy," George McMullen has lent his psychic talents to archaeologists in Canada, the United States, Israel, Egypt, and Iran. "I project myself up in the air," McMullen says, describing his attempts to draw psychic impressions at excavation sites. "I'm looking down on what's going on below as if I were up in a helicopter or perhaps a tall tree." From this perspective, McMullen claims to be able to see things not as they are in the present day, but "as they used to be" in the distant past.

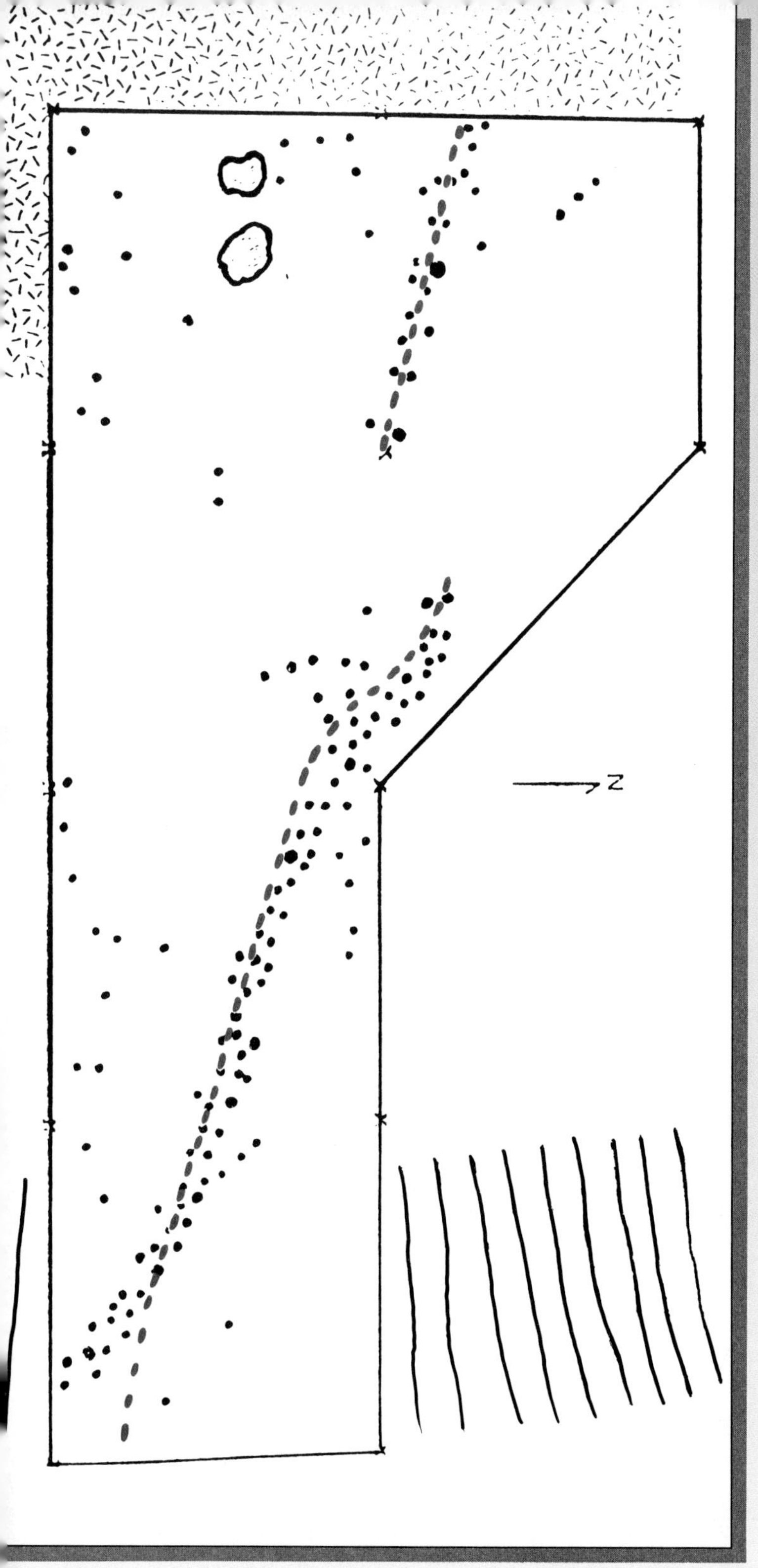

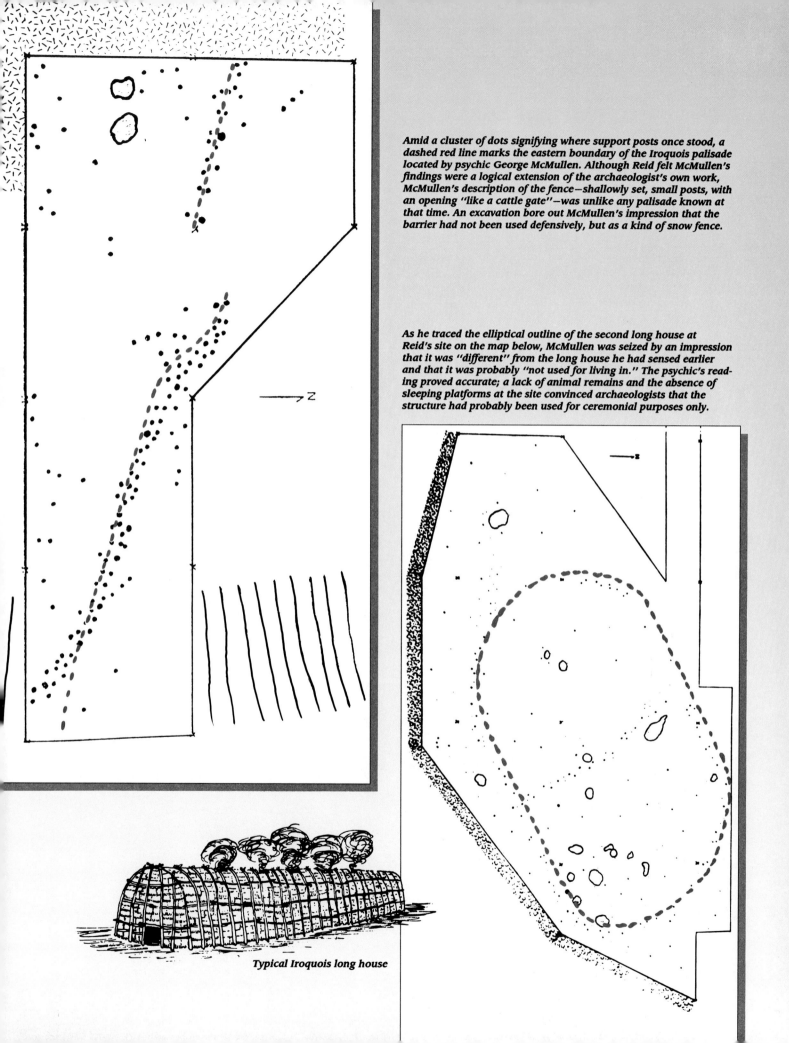

Amid a cluster of dots signifying where support posts once stood, a dashed red line marks the eastern boundary of the Iroquois palisade located by psychic George McMullen. Although Reid felt McMullen's findings were a logical extension of the archaeologist's own work, McMullen's description of the fence—shallowly set, small posts, with an opening "like a cattle gate"—was unlike any palisade known at that time. An excavation bore out McMullen's impression that the barrier had not been used defensively, but as a kind of snow fence.

As he traced the elliptical outline of the second long house at Reid's site on the map below, McMullen was seized by an impression that it was "different" from the long house he had sensed earlier and that it was probably "not used for living in." The psychic's reading proved accurate; a lack of animal remains and the absence of sleeping platforms at the site convinced archaeologists that the structure had probably been used for ceremonial purposes only.

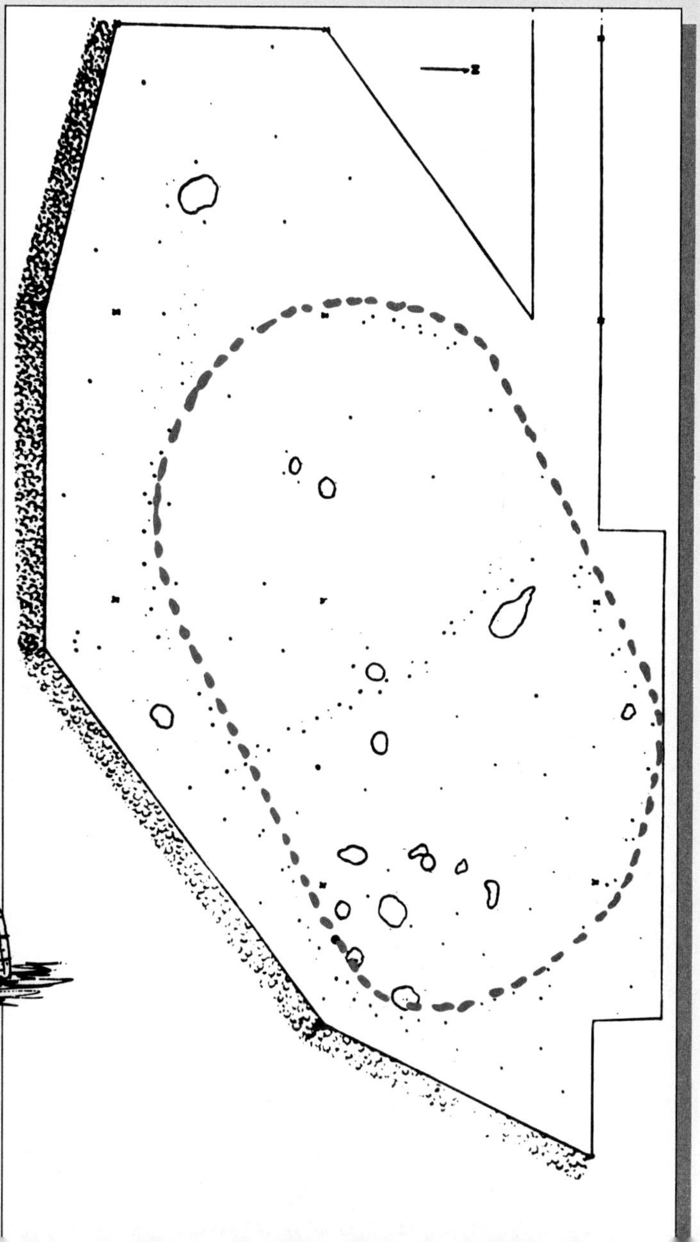

Typical Iroquois long house

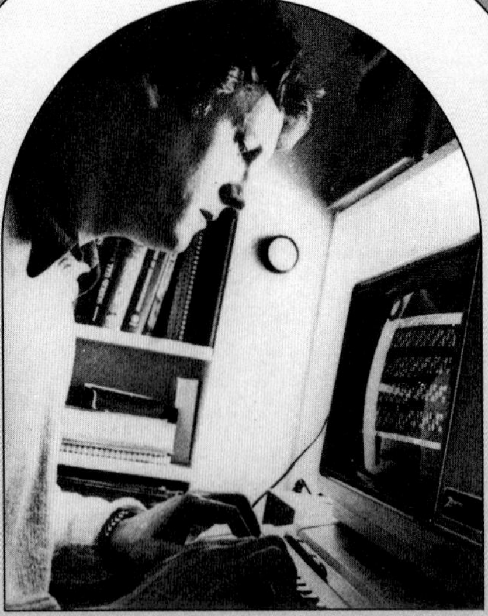

Mobius Society founder Stephan Schwartz

A Test of Powers in Old Egypt

In the fall of 1978, California parapsychologist Stephan Schwartz launched the most ambitious test of psychic abilities ever attempted in archaeology. With a team of twenty-two people, including psychics and conventional scientists, Schwartz traveled to Egypt to prove that paranormal techniques could locate previously unknown sites and artifacts. In the historically rich city of Alexandria, Schwartz declared, his psychic consultants faced the challenge of revealing "not only what we were likely to find, but where to look and how deep down to dig."

Two years earlier, Schwartz had organized a research foundation called the Mobius Society, charged with integrating intuitive methods into the traditional scientific approach to archaeology. Schwartz's strategy called for the participation of several psychics. "In the same way that a journalist would talk to a lot of eyewitnesses, we have several psychics independently picking up the same information," Schwartz explained.

In advance of the Egyptian expedition, Schwartz's behind-the-scenes team of psychic consultants helped him select the general areas he would search. To fine-tune the group's impressions on location, Schwartz brought along a pair of talented seers—German-born Hella Hammid, and Canadian George McMullen, who a few years earlier had helped uncover an Iroquois settlement in Ontario.

Within weeks of their arrival in Egypt, the Mobius team scored a pair of remarkable successes. Beneath the streets of Alexandria, Hammid and McMullen located a long-forgotten Byzantine cistern, and in the buried city of Marea, about forty miles distant, the psychics pinpointed the ruins of a 1,500-year-old building.

For Schwartz, the finds offered proof of what the Mobius Society's talents could do. "Psychic ability is not a cure-all," he admitted, "but neither is it a fraud. Rather, it is a little-understood new tool, to be used not in replacement of, but in conjunction with, traditional scientific research techniques."

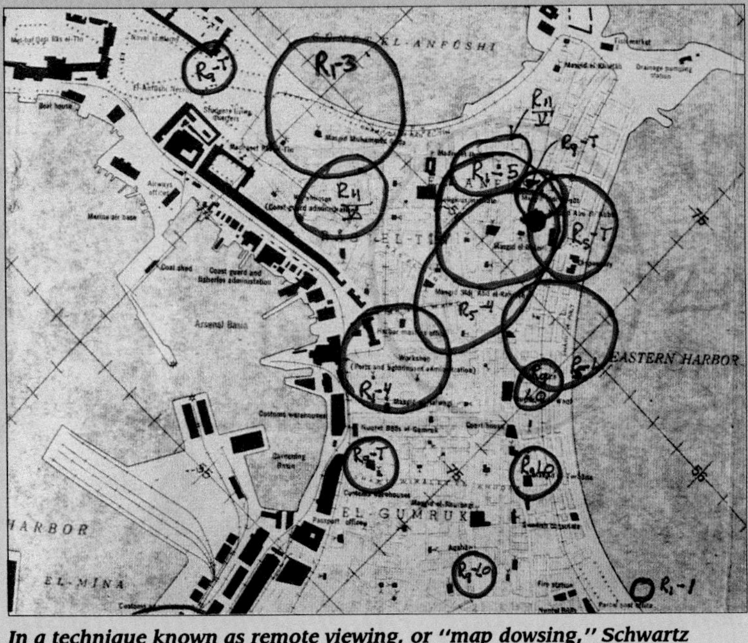

In a technique known as remote viewing, or "map dowsing," Schwartz gave maps of modern Alexandria to eleven independent psychics, who circled areas they sensed were rich in buried artifacts. Where the circles overlapped, as indicated on this composite map, fieldwork was begun.

In Alexandria, Hella Hammid, who credits childbirth with unleashing her psychic instincts, used pencil and paper to record her impressions. Inexplicably, a tape recorder brought along for that purpose repeatedly jammed while she was speaking.

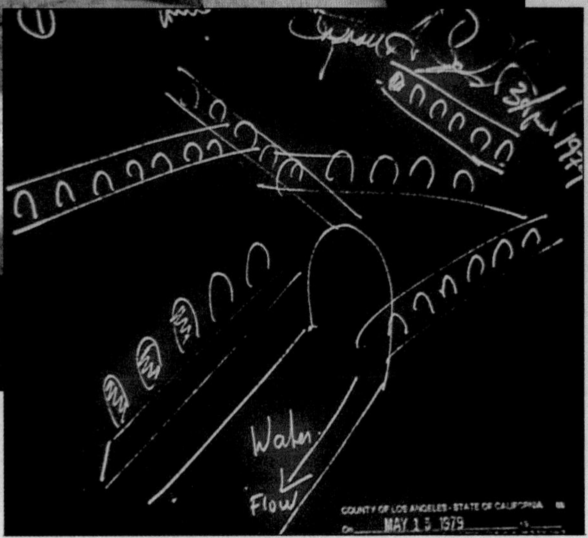

As a colleague looks on, Stephan Schwartz uses a light to examine the long-sealed Byzantine cistern located by the Mobius psychics. In a sketch of her impressions (right), Hella Hammid accurately predicted the multistoried chamber's arched walls and ceilings.

With Stephan Schwartz's help, George McMullen (left) drives a stake at the buried city of Marea, forty miles north of Alexandria, to mark one corner of a building he psychically detected. Out of an area roughly the size of Chicago, both McMullen and Hella Hammid—working separately—chose the same location; both also had impressions of "bathing" and "washing" connected with the site. While the Mobius team's digging uncovered an ancient building within thirty inches of the predictions, they could not confirm that it had been used for bathing. However, a later excavation nearby did unearth a bathhouse.

While McMullen's sketch shows that he misperceived the shape of the marble tiles found at Marea, he accurately described them as smooth on one side and rough on the other. Observed Schwartz, "Out of 225 square miles, he pinpointed the location of an object about the size of a quarter."

This ancient building, whose emerging outline was psychically traced by McMullen, was believed to be Roman until excavation confirmed the seer's impression that the buried structure was Byzantine. Further digging underscored the accuracy of the Mobius psychics: A weathered column (bottom right) foreseen by Hammid and a ledge (inset), whose exact form and depth were described by McMullen, were uncovered.

Wielding straightened coat hangers, Denis Briggs dowses in a church cemetery. He says his talent is "like hearing something . . . a sort of sixth sense."

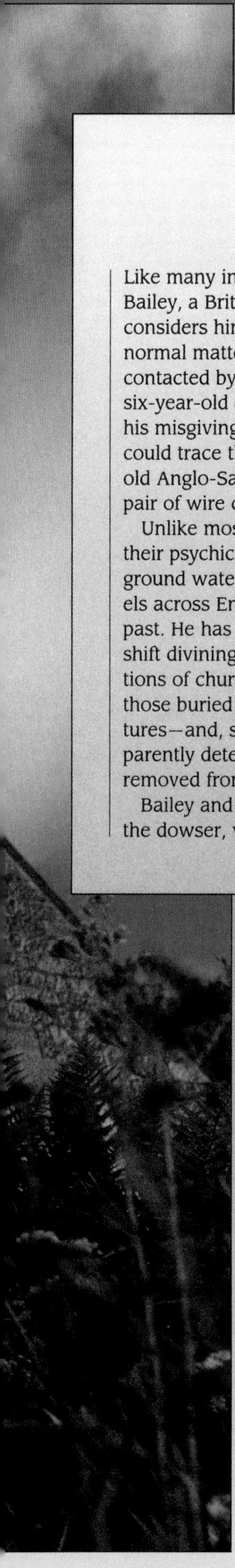

Church archaeologist Richard Bailey

Dowsing for History in an English Churchyard

Like many in his profession, Richard Bailey, a British church archaeologist, considers himself a skeptic about paranormal matters. Yet when he was contacted by Denis Briggs, a seventy-six-year-old dowser, Bailey put aside his misgivings: Briggs claimed he could trace the remains of centuries-old Anglo-Saxon churches using only a pair of wire coat hangers.

Unlike most dowsers, who expend their psychic energy locating underground water or minerals, Briggs travels across England in search of the past. He has reportedly used his makeshift divining rods to trace the foundations of churches long in ruins—even those buried beneath modern structures—and, stranger still, he can apparently detect features that had been removed from the site years earlier.

Bailey and Briggs teamed up when the dowser, who was schooled in engineering, sent detailed plans of his discoveries to Bailey. "I was going to chuck them away, because I get a lot of nutty letters," Bailey later recalled, "but then I noticed that they actually made quite a lot of sense."

Bailey invited Briggs to try his skills at a church in Northumberland. The dowser's divining rods began to trace the outline of a phantom apse—a vaulted, semicircular projection once attached to the church. Bailey brought in other dowsers to confirm Briggs's findings and then started digging. He uncovered a foundation of mortared stones resting a mere inch from where Briggs predicted they would be.

Briggs and Bailey have surveyed eleven church sites, finding hidden features at eight of them. Though Bailey remains cautious, and even slightly embarrassed by such an unorthodox technique, he praises Briggs's dowsing as a nondestructive means of gaining access "to the wealth of untapped material that lies below the floors of parish churches and their surrounding graveyards." The archaeologist suspects that dowsing may already be common among his peers—"although none," he observes wryly, "have admitted as much in print."

Denis Briggs and other dowsers sensed a rectangular object near the altar of this Northumberland church. Later, a set of plans discovered in the local records office revealed that a nineteenth-century altar platform, which exactly matched the dowsers' tracings, had been removed from the site in 1972. The incident seems to contradict widely held views that dowsers only respond to energy fields, or variations in dampness or density below ground. Archaeologist Bailey admits he cannot explain what triggered the dowsers' impressions of a surface object: "I don't see how a wooden platform put in in the 1880s and taken out in the 1970s can still be picked up."

CHAPTER 3

The Holy Grail

The year was 1910, and the men digging a well near the Turkish city of Antakya, or Antioch, had no power equipment to speed their work. They had been at it for some days, backs bent beneath the broiling Mediterranean sun, their progress measured by the piles of excavated earth surrounding them. As they nosed their shovels into the bone-dry soil, they eyed each spadeful of dirt expectantly. A hint of dampness would be cause for joy; an actual trickle would signal success and spell an end to their drudgery.

Suddenly, the eyes of one man caught a glimmer in the dirt. It was not water, but it soon seized the attention of the whole crew. Work stopped as a crowd of hands reached out to help free the find from its crust of earth. It was a pair of cups, one nesting in the other. The inner cup, elegant in its simplicity, was made of some indeterminate metal. The outer one, intricately engraved with grapes and vines and other figures, appeared to be silver.

Although the discovery of such antiquities was hardly unusual in a region that had long cradled civilization, this relic caused a particular stir. No sooner had it found its way into the hands of museum curators and historians than some of those experts dared to ponder the imponderable: Could the inner cup, for all its plainness, be the same cup that had once passed from apostle to apostle at the Last Supper, the cup that purportedly had caught the blood of Christ after the Crucifixion? Was it the same "great and precious vessel," as one chronicler described it, that had spurred the knights of old in quest of enlightenment and eternal life? Might those legends of valor be true after all, and could this cup be the fabled Holy Grail?

The answer came after extensive testing. The results showed that the so-called Antioch Chalice, while old, was not old enough to have played a part in the Last Supper. The vessel could only be dated as far back as the fourth century. But even if science had quashed any hope that this chalice was the Holy Grail, the finding did not preclude the possibility that the much-sought treasure still existed somewhere, nor did it banish the widespread belief that the grail, if found, could bestow wisdom, perpetual youth, and union with the Divine.

For as long as people have been telling each other stories, humanity's quest for immortality, the search for oneness with a deity, and the desire to anchor faith in fact have found expression in myths and legends. Many of the world's oldest stories revolve around a sacred or magical vessel of some kind. In Europe, these ancient, pagan sagas changed in the retelling over the centuries, as the spread of the gospel gradually cloaked the traditions of paganism in the trappings of Christianity. In the process, heathen myth became Christian allegory, its fabric the enduring threads of innocence and fall, temptation and salvation, the despair of losing touch with the Divine, and joyous reunion with the Godhead. In the Holy Grail, all these themes converge.

It is among the most desirable of the world's legendary lost treasures—and certainly one of the most elusive. Even the term *Holy Grail* endures in common parlance as a metaphor for a much-desired benefit, whether sacred or mundane, that is as difficult to attain as it is worth having. An Academy Award, a Harvard law degree, a healthy and happy family—all of these have been referred to as the Holy Grail by people in one walk of life or another. A radio commentator observed in 1991 that the Holy Grail of suburban homeowners is "the perfect lawn."

Of course, for those who quest after the actual Holy Grail, if such an object exists, the stakes are much higher, the task far more serious. Pursuit of the grail has always demanded utter dedication and sacrifice; it defines a hero's life. In virtually all of the old accounts the quester's commitment called forth a character-shaping adventure, laden with ordeals and leavened with the wise, sometimes magical, interventions of hermits and of supernatural beings. Through the centuries in which it has enthralled human imagination, the Holy Grail has inspired many quests and tales of quests—and, occasionally, it still does. As much spiritual odyssey as physical pilgrimage, the quest has offered the hope of spiritual perfection in this life and, ultimately, of union with the Divine. Personages of grail lore, which is a mixture of legend, religious belief, and history, include King Arthur and his Knights of the Round Table, Joseph of Arimathea, the Queen of Sheba, untold thousands of Crusaders, and even Adolf Hitler. For many of them, as for countless others now forgotten, the grail became a way of life or an obsession, delivering or promising unsurpassed blessings.

Since no object has been found that experts can agree to call the Holy Grail, only the stories about it present themselves for examination—and they are multifarious. In the many versions of the tale, both spoken and written, diverse traditions have overlapped and intertwined, and details have been exchanged, embellished, added, and omitted from one telling to the next. To discern the elements of fact that survive in this tangle of folklore and history has become as difficult a prospect as finding the grail itself.

Not least of the mysteries that shroud the Holy Grail is the confusion regarding its exact form. Part pagan talisman and part Christian relic, the grail earned its place in literature as the will-o'-the-wisp of medieval romances, and in history as an enigma. Its whereabouts were said to be the jealously guarded secret of a chosen few and its very existence a continuing cause of conjecture. Although many of the legends agree that the Holy Grail is a repository of superhuman power and divine truth, those same stories may differ dramatically on the grail's very form. Most often, the grail is understood to be the chalice used by Christ at

the Last Supper. Some grail researchers, however, have depicted the treasure as a precious stone or as an emerald loosed from the crown of Lucifer during his fateful struggle with God. Still others have imagined it as a magic cauldron, as a platter bearing a severed human head, or even as the womb of the Virgin Mary. More recently, some theorists have argued that the grail was an elaborate storage chest for the Shroud of Turin—the alleged burial cloth of Christ—or, pursuing a wild notion seemingly designed to offend the faithful, that it was the child fathered by Jesus Christ in a secret coupling with Mary Magdalene.

Given the variety of the Holy Grail legends, it is hardly surprising that the grail itself exhibited such a markedly split personality. One authority, American scholar Roger S. Loomis, observed that "the authors of the Grail texts seem to delight in contradicting each other on the most important points." For all its multiplicity of forms, however, and despite its longstanding association with Christianity, the

The Lure of a Sacred Image

"One must have an explanation for the image of the Shroud which is scientifically sound. This type of solution does not appear to be obtainable by the best efforts of the Shroud Team." So wrote the authors of a report on the Shroud of Turin after a 1978 investigation. In short, they admitted that science could not account for the mysterious likeness imprinted on the mantle, which has drawn attention for centuries.

A linen sheet fourteen feet long and three and a half feet wide, the shroud displays in a faint brown tint the face and body image of a bearded man. Reddish stains dot the figure's left side, wrists, feet, and head—places where Jesus bled from the wounds of torture and crucifixion. When the cloth is photographed, a curious phenomenon occurs: The photo negative *(far right)* reveals the Christ-like image much more clearly than the positive print *(near right).*

The shroud first appeared among France's crowd-pulling Christian relics in 1354, when a destitute nobleman, Geoffrey de Charny, charged admission from those wishing to view it. He declared that it was Christ's death wrap, imprinted with the very features of the crucified Lord. The sheet changed hands over the ensuing centuries, coming to rest in 1578 at the cathedral in the Italian city of Turin. A chapel was erected for it, and millions of worshipers have made pilgrimages there just to gaze enrapt upon the protective silver case in which the cloth is enclosed.

In 1988, cathedral authorities allowed scientists to use swatches of the shroud for a carbon-14 test. Results indicated it did not date from the time of Christ—from no earlier, in fact, than the Middle Ages. Despite that seemingly incontrovertible debunking, some people still revere the cloth as the only remaining authentic relic of Jesus Christ.

Nor is the matter settled, entirely. The 1988 investigation failed to address the mystery of how the image of a crucified man might have appeared upon a piece of linen hundreds of years before the advent of photography. Scientists have ruled out both artifice and all known natural processes as the cause. The faithful chalk it up to a miracle.

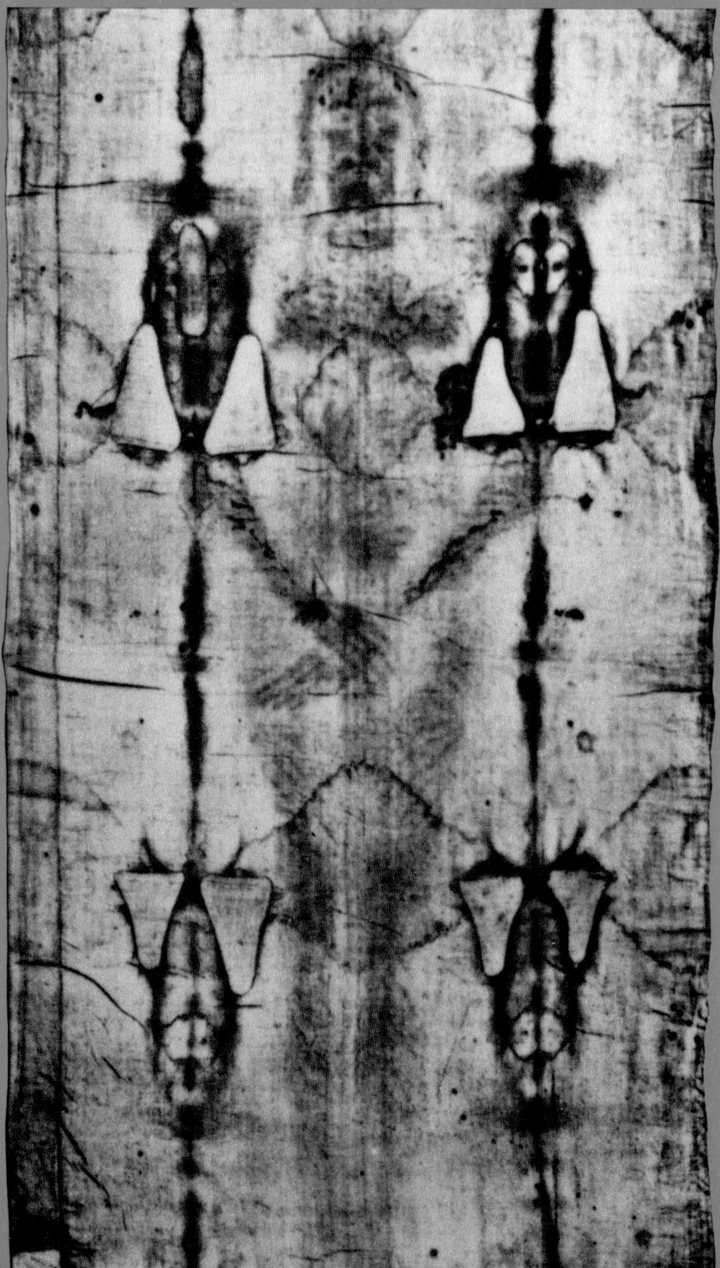

grail has deep and ancient roots in pagan mythology.

Many Celtic myths, for example, are set in a dreamy otherworld, where heroes and nobles satisfy their appetites and slake their thirsts on limitless amounts of food and drink supplied in a variety of vessels or horns of plenty. In some instances, the cornucopia takes the form of a dish, such as the celebrated platter of Rhydderch the Generous, by means of which any food could reportedly be conjured up at will. More often, the vessel is described as a cauldron endowed with magical powers. The Celtic god Goibniu, for one, supposedly used such a cauldron to brew a beer that rendered its imbibers immortal, while Dagda, Irish folklore's Father of the Gods, was said to have a pot that would cook food only for heroes.

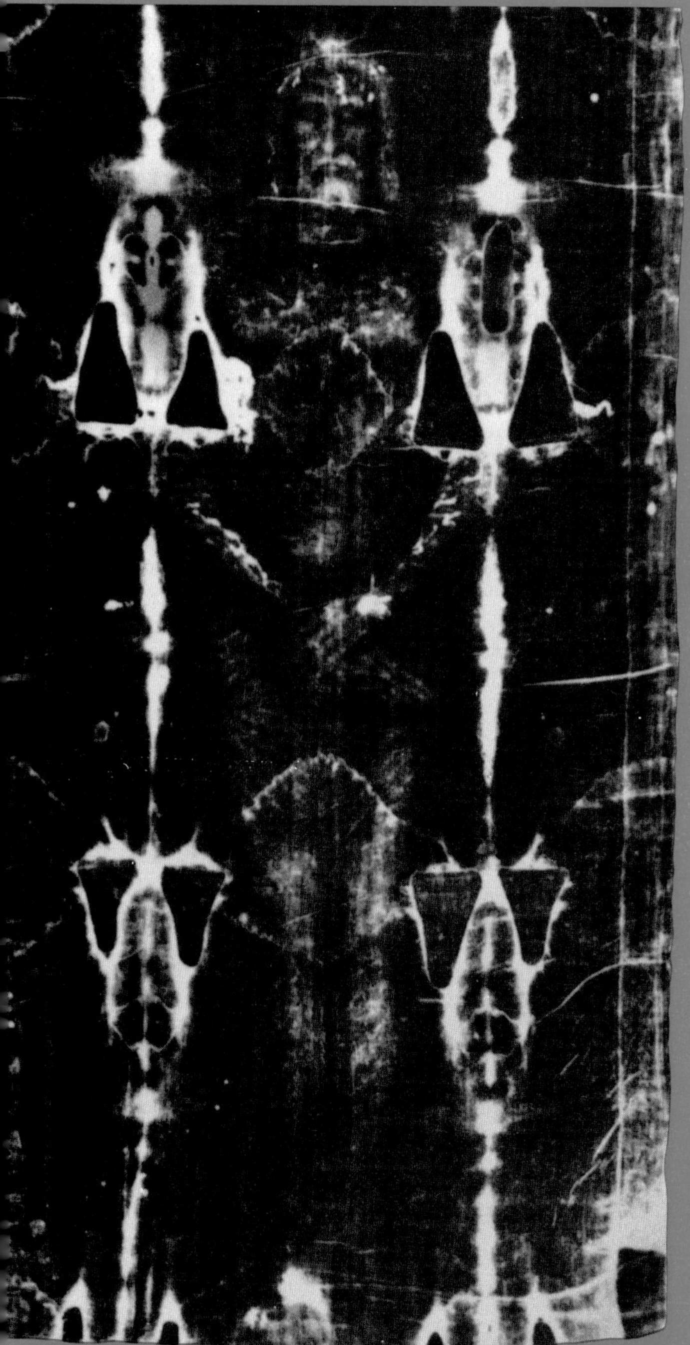

More magical still was the man-size cauldron described in *The Mabinogion,* a collection of Welsh legends. This exemplary vessel, belonging to the Celtic hero Bran the Blessed, allegedly had the power to restore the dead to life. "A man of thine slain today," advises *The Mabinogion,* "cast him into the cauldron, and by tomorrow he will be as well as he was at the best, save only that he will not have power of speech."

These Celtic cauldrons of rebirth and plenty had their classical counterparts in Greek mythology and philosophy. In his *Psychogony,* the philosopher Plato described two such vessels in the domain of the deity who created the universe. In one pot, the god mixed what Plato called "the All-Soul of Universal Nature," and from the other the creator "ladled out the minds of men." And the *Corpus Hermeticum,* ascribed to Greek god and prophet Hermes Trismegistus, tells of a divine cup, or krater, in which an all-powerful deity stirred together the elements of life. From this cosmic mixing bowl, each newly created soul was supposedly permitted to gulp down its allotment of intelligence and wisdom.

Together, the magical powers of the Celtic cauldron and the mystical contents of the Greek krater seem to have provided a major ingredient of the grail legends. In fact, the variety of these ancient vessels of bounty and renewal—whether cup or cauldron, platter, horn, or krater—may account for later confusion regarding the shape of the grail. All that was needed was the arrival of Christianity and the glow of chivalry to transform these pagan talismans into the Holy Grail, the Christian symbol of spiritual renewal.

The idea of a sacred vessel was not the only Celtic contribution to the grail legends. From the Celts, too, came the inspiration to put the grail into the hands of a protector, or grail keeper, and to remove this person or supernatural being to a mysterious sanctuary known as the Grail Castle.

From these threads of tradition the authors of the grail legends wove a fascinating mythology. Some of the legends that make up this mythology are more elaborate than others, but most of them feature a crippled monarch known as the Fisher King. As the guardian of the Holy Grail, the Fisher King lives in a magnificent castle, but his dominion has been ravaged by a terrible drought. Into this so-called Waste Land comes a wandering knight, whose arrival prompts the Fisher King to order a lavish feast. During the festivities the grail appears, carried in a procession. The knight, though baffled by the curious events, stifles the urge to question his host and, in doing so, unwittingly fails a test that has been set for him. He later learns that had he only asked a simple question—such as "Whom does the Grail serve?" or "Uncle, what ails thee?"—the king would have been healed, the Waste Land restored, and the mystery of the grail revealed.

In tracing this story to its source, scholars have noted a resemblance between the Fisher King and Celtic strongman Bran the Blessed, owner of the cauldron that supposedly restored the dead to life. According to the Celtic myth, Bran was a giant, so large that no house could hold him and so powerful that few men dared to challenge him. He was, moreover, the son of Llyr, the Celtic god of the sea, and he was said to have died after being wounded in the foot by a poisoned spear. On his own instructions, Bran's head was severed after his death and ensconced in a great hall, where it served as an apparently effective, though grisly, talisman. Thanks to its magical powers, Bran's companions were reportedly wined and dined for the next eighty years, during which time none of the merrymakers aged a single day.

How the legend of Bran contributed to the story of the Fisher King is apparent, not only in the common images of a wounded leader and a sumptuous feast, but also in the symbolism of a severed human head. The head was worshiped by the Celts as the seat of the soul and referred to as the Holy Grail in some of the later legends. The link can also be seen in certain legends that tell of the grail being buried on a mountaintop, or of a feast attended by knights who had never aged beyond their prime. Most striking of all is the similarity between the name Bran and that of Bron, one of the more frequently mentioned characters in the later grail legends. Bron is sometimes identified as the brother-in-law of Joseph of Arimathea, the man who provided a tomb for Jesus' burial and allegedly the original caretaker of the grail. Bron is also associated with the Fisher King, having earned his nickname by mysteriously feeding his followers with a single fish that he took from the grail.

A mysterious nocturnal visitor plunges his spear through the Fisher King's thigh in the symbolic castration that begins the Holy Grail legend. Storytellers made the tale of the wounded ruler parallel that of Jesus' death and Resurrection: The lance-bearing attacker is probably based on the biblical Roman centurion who pierced the side of Christ on the cross.

Bron's ability to stretch a meal, through the auspices of the Holy Grail, quite obviously echoes Christ's miraculous feeding of the five thousand, and clearly reflects Christianity's influence on the many legends surrounding the grail. Indeed, by the time the legends were first written down, beginning in the second half of the twelfth century, Christianity had already commandeered many of the old pagan myths. Later versions of the stories would show an increasing reliance on Christian themes and symbols. Some of the most beloved of the grail stories were those told by medieval romancers. Among these are some that recount the quintessential quests—the adventures of King Arthur and his Knights of the Round Table.

The Arthurian grail legends first appeared in Europe during the latter part of the twelfth century. The oldest surviving record of the tale is *Le Conte du Graal,* or *The Story of the Grail,* written around 1180 by the French poet Chrétien de Troyes. Chrétien brought together such traditional story elements as the Fisher King and the wandering knight—to whom he gave the name Perceval—with new plot features such as a hermit who admonished the knight to "believe in God, love God, worship God." The tales of the quests made by Arthur's heroes were then told and retold, written and rewritten by a succession of medieval troubadours, chroniclers, poets, bards, monks, and mystics, so that by the end of the thirteenth century, virtually everyone on the Continent was familiar with the stirring adventures.

How much of Chrétien's original poem was the product of his own imagination and how much he borrowed from tradition is impossible to know. What is clear is that the poet went out of his way to present his story as fact rather than fiction. He credited a long-vanished prose version of the story as the source of his inspiration, and he thanked Count Philip of Flanders for the suggestion that he put the tale to rhyme.

In the opinion of at least one eminent scholar—mythologist Joseph Campbell—the grail legend reached its richest expression in the work of Wolfram von Eschenbach. Wolfram was a Bavarian poet, a knight, and a mystic who wrote his greatest work, *Parzifal,* sometime before 1207. Given his vocation as a courtly man-at-arms, Wolfram understood, as did no other chronicler before him, both the religious motives of the legend and the chivalric code that governed the life and aspirations of a knight.

Wolfram called his hero Parzifal, the German version of Perceval, although the hero is French. Cast as the "perfect fool," this character would be at the heart of all the great Arthurian legends to come. He would feature most notably in Sir Thomas Malory's classic *Morte d'Arthur.*

Wolfram set his narrative in his own time, the period of the Crusades, when Christian armies laid siege to the Middle East at the urging of Pope Urban II. The tale begins with an account of Parzifal's father, Gahmuret, a noble fellow who has set as his goal perfect spiritual knighthood. In the service of the caliph of Baghdad, a prince of Islam, Gahmuret happens one day on the castle of Queen Belacane. The queen, as it turns out, is in quite a predicament with her fortress under siege by two separate armies, one Muslim and one Christian. Gahmuret brings the sieges to an end and marries the grateful Belacane, who is described by Wolfram as "black as night." The couple have a son named Feirefiz, who is both black and white, but Gahmuret soon tires of domestic life and makes his way back to Europe. There, a young queen named Herzeloyde has organized a jousting match in which she offers herself as the prize. Gahmuret wins the meet and marries the young queen, who is as fair as Belacane was dark. They too have a son, and they give him the name Parzifal. Soon afterward, on a visit to Baghdad, Gahmuret is killed in battle.

Parzifal's widowed mother chooses to rear her son in the countryside, far from the world of armies and knights that took her husband. But when Parzifal chances to meet a group of knights from Arthur's court and hears of the great happenings at the Round Table, he is filled with determination to serve the fabled monarch. Herzeloyde tries to dampen her son's dreams of heroism by sewing for him a robe suitable only for a fool. But the boy takes little notice of the clothing as he puts it on, mounts the farm horse, and rides away, leaving Herzeloyde to die of her grief.

Parzifal proceeds straightaway to King Arthur's court and happens to arrive just moments before a formidable-looking warrior in red armor. When this other newcomer offends the honor of Queen Guinevere and invites her defenders to meet him on the field of battle, Parzifal does not hesitate. The red knight regards this adversary, still riding his plow horse and dressed in fool's robe, and he can do little more than laugh. Clutching the tip of his lance, he uses the butt end to swat Parzifal off his shambling mount. The youth, ignorant of the niceties of jousting, then hurls his javelin through the visor of the red knight's helmet, killing him on the spot. The boy dons the dead knight's armor, mounts his fine horse, and rides away.

That evening, Parzifal is so fortunate as to be taken in at the castle of Gurnemanz, an old knight who has lived alone with his daughter since his three sons were killed on the jousting field. Recognizing a diamond in the rough,

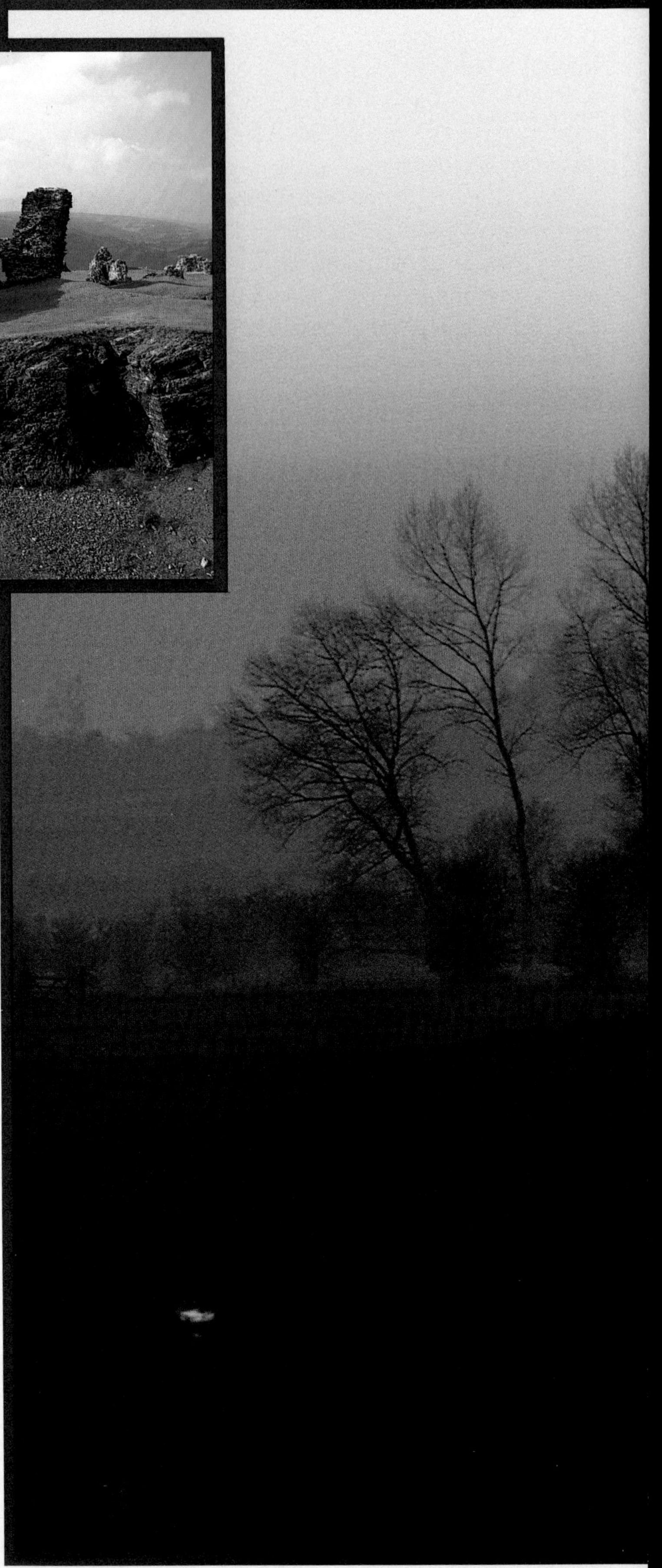

Castle Dinas Brân (inset), one-time stronghold of the Celtic King Bran, lies a crumpled ruin in northern Wales. Legend tells that Bran's grail-like cauldron could feed 500 people, provided none was a coward. Some believe the magical vessel is still hidden in the rubble of the fortress. Others are certain, however, that the true grail resides beneath the slopes of Glastonbury Tor (right), in southwestern England.

Sir Gurnemanz offers to instruct Parzifal in the arts and skills of knighthood—an offer the young man gladly accepts. Throughout the many lessons that ensue, one of Gurnemanz's watchwords is discretion. "Do not ask too many questions," he advises. Parzifal proves so accomplished a student that the old knight is moved to offer his daughter's hand in marriage. Parzifal hesitates, then politely declines, saying: "No; I must earn my bride, not be given her."

The young knight rides away, letting his horse choose the way, and comes to the castle of Condwiramurs, an orphaned queen of about his own age, whose name means "guide to love." He is received with the customary hospitality afforded knights in those days, but in the middle of the night he is awakened by Condwiramurs's weeping, and he finds the young queen kneeling at his bedside. "Do not kneel," he gently counsels, "to anybody but God." He then inquires about the cause of her unhappiness and is told that a king whom Condwiramurs dislikes has demanded her hand in marriage. The next day, Parzifal challenges a knight in the service of the unwelcome suitor to a joust and swiftly unseats him from his horse. Now fully conversant with knightly ways, Parzifal orders this foe to go to Arthur's court and tell of his defeat. And in the months that follow, many other vanquished knights make the same trip, all of them attesting to Parzifal's prowess.

In the meantime, Condwiramurs has bound up her hair in the manner of a married woman, and the pair consummate their love. By the time the queen gives birth to the first of his two sons, Parzifal has become a renowned knight and is in the fullness of life. He is ready—in Wolfram's view—for a spiritual adventure. Thus, Parzifal sets out once again, letting the reins lie slack on his horse's neck. This time, the steed carries him to a lake in the barren, drought-stricken kingdom of the Waste Land.

On the lake is a boat in which two men sit fishing, one

The ruined Takt-i-Suleiman, a temple in Iran, vies with Glastonbury, Castle Dinas Brän, and numerous other sites for status as the Grail Castle. The shrine became a candidate in the mid-twentieth century, when scholars found an allusion to an Eastern grail sanctuary in a medieval German poem.

of whom bears a grievous wound that will never heal. This is the Fisher King—called the Grail King in Wolfram's tale because he has been assigned to safeguard the sacred relic. Some time ago, Parzifal learns, the king had ridden forth in search of love and adventure. In doing so, he had violated his calling to protect the grail, and he had paid a terrible price for this transgression. In the course of his travels, he had met and challenged a pagan knight and had succeeded in killing the enemy. But he had been castrated in the process and had ridden painfully back to his castle with the tip of a lance still embedded in the wound. When the weapon was at last removed, the king saw the words The Grail written on it. His injuries could not kill him, because he was under the protection of the grail. But he was nearly without hope that they would ever heal, and his land had lost its ability to flower.

Now, as the Grail King sits in his boat, he knows that the only cure for his predicament is what Joseph Campbell called "the spontaneous act of a noble heart, moved by compassion." Hailed by the wandering Parzifal, he invites the knight to partake of a generous feast at his castle. The king and all his retinue are under an enchantment and, in the usual way of magical stories, they know what must be done to break free of the spell but are themselves powerless to do it. Parzifal, on the other hand, has it in his power to free them, but he has no idea what steps might be necessary.

The Grail King is carried into the banquet hall on a litter, but he cannot rest with any comfort because of his wounds. Seeing his suffering, Parzifal wishes to ask, "Uncle, what ails thee?" But he remembers Gurnemanz's admonition not to ask too many questions, so he keeps silent. All around him, the people of the Waste Land know that a great opportunity has been lost. The Grail King graciously presents Parzifal with a sword but notes that it will probably break at a critical moment.

When Parzifal awakes in the morning, his horse has been readied for him. He mounts and rides out of the castle, barely leaving the drawbridge before it rises behind him. For the next five years, he will search in vain for the castle he has just departed. But even when it sits right beside him, his eyes are not capable of seeing it. And all the while, the brave men of Arthur's court have been searching for the noble Sir Parzifal.

One morning, Parzifal sees the black feathers and red blood of a dead crow lying in the snow. He is reminded of the black hair, white skin, and red lips of his beloved Condwiramurs, and he falls into a trance. A page from Arthur's entourage spies the motionless knight and reports the sighting to Arthur. Sir Gawain is sent to fetch the stranger and, being a knight with much worldly experience, he recognizes a love trance when he sees one. Sir Gawain tosses his yellow kerchief in front of Parzifal's eyes, and the spell is broken. Parzifal says, "Greetings to Arthur's Court."

As Arthur and his subjects feast with their guest, a most unusual woman approaches, riding on a mule. She has the face of a boar, the hands of a monkey, and a fashionable hat slung from her neck. Identifying herself as the Grail Messenger, she mocks Parzifal, saying: "You are more ugly than I, despite the beauty of your face." The lady then tells the story of Parzifal's failure at the court of the Grail King and warns that the knight has been cursed by God.

Although it may also have housed the grail, the Takt-i-Suleiman, depicted here on a seventh-century tray, was built as a temple for a cross alleged to be the one on which Christ was crucified. The Persian king Khosrow II had stolen the relic during a sack of Jerusalem.

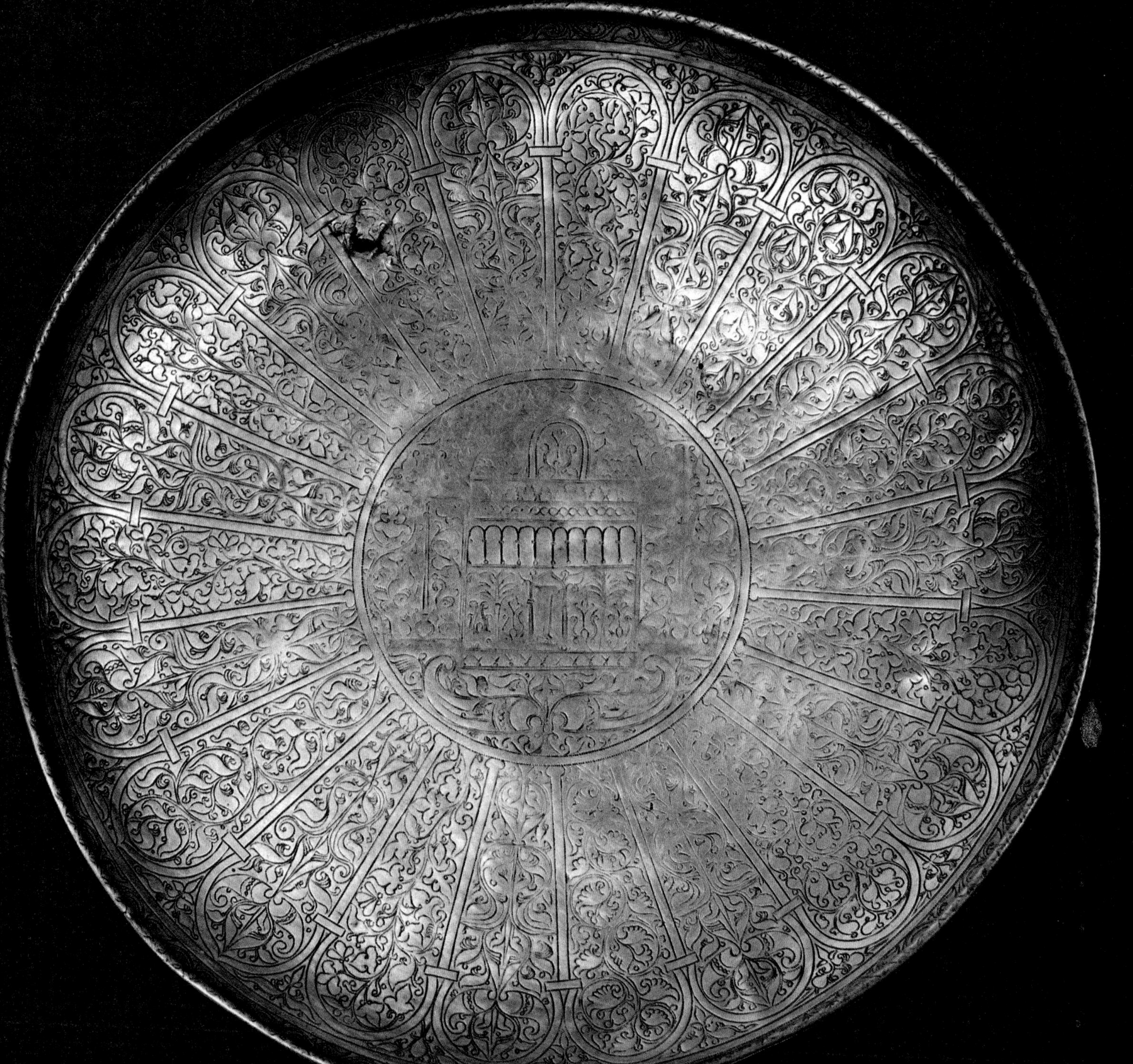

Iron-rich water from the Chalice Well in Glastonbury (below) spouts out of a nearby carved lion's head (left), staining the stones beneath. Some believe the grail is hidden in the well and that traces of Christ's blood within the holy cup account for the reddish residue that the water leaves behind.

The woebegone knight then departs Arthur's court and resumes his life of wandering. A hermit named Trevortsent shares a meal with him and suggests that they offer a prayer before eating. "I don't say grace," replies Parzifal, "I hate God." "But God," says the hermit, "returns manyfold what you give to him—be it love or hate." Parzifal then describes his adventure with the Fisher King and declares that he is going back to remedy his error. The hermit tells him sorrowfully that he is attempting the impossible, but Parzifal insists that he will never stop trying.

The next time Parzifal visits Arthur's court, he arrives in the middle of Sir Gawain's marriage celebration, and he engages the bridegroom in a jousting competition that ends with both competitors being unseated. His honor somewhat restored, Parzifal is invited to join the feasting, but he is still too overwrought to take part in the merriment. As he is about to leave, he encounters a pagan knight, and the two are at once locked in mortal combat. When Parzifal's sword—the one given to him by the Grail King—breaks in the heat of battle, the pagan knight suddenly has the upper hand but gallantly throws his own weapon away. Sitting down together, the two knights draw off their helmets, and the adversary is revealed to be none other than Parzifal's half-brother, Feirefiz. Together, they take part in the marriage celebration.

Once again the Grail Messenger appears, this time saying to Parzifal: "Come to the Grail castle. Through your loyalty, you have achieved the adventure. And bring your pagan friend." At the castle, the grail—in this account, a precious stone—is borne in by a beautiful virgin. Parzifal turns to the Grail King and at last asks the crucial question, "What ails you, Uncle?" The king is healed and waters are released to flow again through the parched Waste Land. Life and fertility return, and the Grail King, released from the curse, is at last able to die. Parzifal inherits the Grail Castle and takes his place as its new lord. Presently Condwiramurs arrives with the new king's two sons, and they all enjoy a tender reunion.

Wolfram's long poem, like the other medieval versions of the grail legend, was part of an ongoing process in which relatively new Christian ideas were married to old pagan traditions. But there was even more to it than that. As was the custom for writers of his time, Wolfram cited a source for his story, naming an author called Kyot der Provenzal as his principal authority. This Kyot, or Guiot, may have been the French troubadour Guiot de Provins or perhaps Guillot of Tudela, who wrote part of a work called the *Chanson de la Croisade albigeoise.* Wolfram claimed, moreover, that his source had relied on an Arabic manuscript by "the heathen Flegetanis," a Jewish astronomer in Toledo, Spain, at a time when that city was a hotbed of alchemical research.

Wolfram's reliance on a writer who was quite possibly involved in alchemy would explain why he envisioned the grail not as a chalice but as "a stone of the purest kind." This sounds suspiciously like a reference to the philosophers' stone—the elusive substance, whether powder or crystal, that was the goal of all true alchemists. Indeed, Wolfram claimed for the grail powers similar to those that the alchemists attributed to the philosophers' stone. Both allegedly gave to their possessors spiritual perfection, union with God, and release from the fear of death. "Such power does the stone give a man that flesh and bones are at once made young again," Wolfram wrote in *Parzifal.*

On the other hand, Wolfram also records that the grail was carved from a particular precious stone, an emerald that had fallen from Lucifer's crown during his fateful battle with God. The Arabic manuscript that Wolfram cites in attributing the ideas contained in his book may have been the source of his knowledge of Persian legends regarding this momentous struggle. The legends suggest that when God decided to expel Lucifer from heaven, the angels were forced to take sides and chose either God or the devil. But there were a few neutral angels, who refused to fall in with either camp. And when Lucifer lost his emerald, they were the ones who brought the stone to earth. There it was to serve as an emblem of the struggle to find a middle way in this life—to locate the middle ground between good and evil, between fear and desire. Wolfram notes that the name Perceval comes from the French *per ce val,* or "right through the valley." The name therefore signifies a person who finds his way between opposites.

Wolfram's use of his primary source, the mysterious poet from Provence in the south of France, seems to announce in a very subtle way another of his philosophical foundations. At the beginning of the thirteenth century, the region that included Provence and neighboring Languedoc was not only a great cultural center but also a stronghold for such Christian splinter groups as the Albigenses, or Cathars, and the Knights Templars. Wolfram was apparently sympathetic to both of these movements, but it was dangerous to broadcast such views at the time. His support for the Cathars and Knights Templars was carefully concealed because the Catholic church was in the habit of dealing very harshly with its enemies.

According to Wolfram, the grail drew its power from a sacred host—in his words, "a small white wafer" placed upon it each Good Friday by "a dove winging down from Heaven." The grail, in turn, sustained the lives of a brotherhood of chaste knights, called the Templeisen, by pouring forth an abundance of "food warm or food cold, dishes new or old, meat tame or game." Both in name and by reputation, Wolfram's fictional Templeisen mirrored the historical Knights Templars, members of a secret order of monkish knights formed during the early part of the twelfth century. The order grew from a core of nine knights who had dedicated themselves to escorting pilgrims safely to Jerusalem during the time of the Crusades. Their way of life centered on vows of poverty, chastity, and humility—rules spelled out by Saint Bernard of Clairvaux, one of the great spiritual leaders of the Cistercian order of monks.

Despite their vows, the Knights Templars consolidated power and wealth over the next two centuries, until they came to be viewed as a threat by the very church they had sworn to uphold. In the end they were accused of heresy and crushed by kings and princes across Western Europe in response to a papal edict.

Like their real-life counterparts, who made their home in a palace near the site of Solomon's Temple, the Templeisen were headquartered in a castle. Wolfram's fictional stronghold was called Munsalvaesche, or "mountain of salvation," a name that echoes that of Montségur, the mountain stronghold of the Cathars in Languedoc. Like the Knights Templars, the Cathars would eventually be denounced as heretics.

The Cathars repudiated the cross, believing that Jesus' death could not have been enough to raise humankind from its wretched state. They viewed all creation as the work of the devil and regarded life on earth as a battle between evil and good. Adopting a rigorously upright life—their name means "the pure"—they taught that each person must struggle alone in hopes of achieving salvation. However, the grim asceticism of the Cathars was relieved by the spiritually revolutionary belief that anyone who so desired could have a direct relationship with God. In Wolfram's poem, Parzifal's long quest to set things right in his life seems to mirror this teaching. Finding his own way at every step, the knight ultimately succeeds in meeting God on his own terms.

Wolfram's not-so-veiled references to the Cathars sparked contemporary speculation that he was himself a member of the sect. This connection, coupled with the Templeisen's resemblance to the Knights Templars and the fact that the author set his story in his own time, brought the grail story right up to date for many of Wolfram's readers. No doubt, this sense of the timeliness of *Parzifal* served to perpetuate the belief that the Holy Grail still existed.

In his famous poem, Wolfram did not address the question of how the grail had come to be in Europe in the first place. That question was addressed by an English poet, Robert de Borron, in his own lengthy work called *Joseph d'Arimathie.*

Borron, like Wolfram, prefaces his poem with an acknowledgment of his debt to an earlier source—in this case, a nameless "great book" written by equally anonymous "great clerks." *Joseph d'Arimathie,* he claims, was given to

Wearing a red tunic and guided by a monk, Galahad appears before King Arthur and his companions at Camelot. In the medieval story Queste del Saint Graal, the young knight completes the Round Table's reenactment of the Last Supper by taking the Siege Perilous—the seat of Judas. In the tale, Galahad's purity allows him to fulfill this otherwise treacherous duty without harm befalling the group. And he wins the respect of the older men, who "did their best to honour and serve him, accounting him master and lord of all their fellowship."

him by an angel or even, perhaps, by Christ himself. Once plundered of its contents, the work supposedly vanished. The poet may have also consulted a pair of Apocryphal texts, the so-called Gospel of Nicodemus and the Acts of Pilate, which divulged many of the same details found in Borron's version of the legend.

Whatever its sources, *Joseph d'Arimathie* has as its centerpiece a grail that was not only the cup passed around at the Last Supper, but also the vessel used to capture Christ's blood after the Crucifixion. According to Borron, the resurrected Jesus appeared to a tin merchant named Joseph of Arimathea—the same wealthy man who had provided the tomb for Christ's burial—and asked him to be the guardian of the Holy Grail, an honor that would fall to his family in perpetuity. In identifying the grail as the chalice of the Last Supper and linking it directly to Christ through Joseph of Arimathea, Borron enhanced the Christian significance of both the object and the legends surrounding it.

As Borron's story unfolds, Joseph flees Palestine with a handful of followers, including his sister and her husband, Bron. It is Bron who, upon Joseph's death, will inherit custody of the Holy Grail and become the first in a line of Fisher Kings. During his exile, Joseph establishes a ritual involving a table that pays homage to the Last Supper. Called the First Table of the Grail, the ritual involves setting twelve places around a table with a fish, the traditional symbol of Christ,

A white stag and his company of lions lead the Arthurian grail seekers safely out of a labyrinthine forest as a hermit monk—the men's spiritual guide—looks on. The iconography in this fifteenth-century painting confirms that the legends of King Arthur linked the tenets of Christianity with the quest for the grail. The stag symbolizes both Christ and the soul's desire for God, while the lions represent the Resurrection.

placed at the table's head. A thirteenth seat, representing that of the traitor Judas, is kept empty. This last detail supposedly dates from the time when one of Joseph's followers sat in the chair and was immediately swallowed up by the earth. The unlucky thirteenth seat would come to be called the Siege Perilous and would be reserved for the descendants of Bron, who presumably were pure enough to sit in the chair without incurring disaster.

For seekers of the Holy Grail, purity thus became a central theme and a prime requisite, and this new element of the tradition made room for the introduction of a new character. He took shape in the person of Sir Galahad, in the *Queste del Saint Graal,* a work composed sometime before 1225 but later than *Parzifal* and *Joseph d'Arimathie.* This updated version of the Arthurian events completed the transformation of the Holy Grail into a spiritual icon. The new narrative was probably the work of Cistercian monks, the spiritual descendants of Saint Bernard of Clairvaux.

In keeping with its monastic origins, the *Queste del Saint Graal* presents the quest as more than a search for a sacred object in hopes of acquiring the attendant blessings. "No search for earthly things," the quest becomes a struggle to achieve mystical union with God—it is "a seeking out of the mysteries of our Lord, the divine secrets which the most high Master will disclose." In this context, the grail is now construed as containing "those things that the heart of mortal man cannot conceive nor tongue relate."

As the man who can pursue such a quest, pure and virginal Galahad is introduced to the ranks of Arthur's knights. He is the son of Lancelot and a man "so grounded in the love of Christ that no adventure can tempt him into sin." Among all the knights, only Galahad will survive to peer into the Holy Grail and comprehend its secrets.

Set out in detail in the *Queste del Saint Graal,* the adventures of Galahad and his companion knights are also recounted in Malory's *Morte d'Arthur.* A fixture in both of these books—as in earlier tellings of the legend—is Perceval, here dubbed the Perfect Fool. In these books, Perceval is a full member of King Arthur's court, as are Galahad, humble Sir Bors, powerful Gawain, and Galahad's father, Lancelot. They take up their quest after the grail miraculously appears before the king and his company on the feast of Pentecost. In a scene strikingly similar to the biblical account of the first Pentecost—when the Holy Spirit descended on the gathered apostles—Arthur and his knights are struck dumb, as a peal of thunder heralds the arrival of the grail. The vessel floats regally into the great hall of Camelot swathed in silk, its path marked by "a sunbeam more clear by seven times than ever they saw day."

Transfixed by this vision, the knights pledge themselves at once to pursue the quest and gallop from Camelot in hopes of another brief glimpse of the grail. Trials await each knight, however, and few of Arthur's stalwarts will ever again set eyes on the grail. Lancelot, blinded by his fatal passion for Guinevere, falters and fails the quest, as does Gawain, who had pinned all his hopes on his own human strength rather than asking God for help. One by one, the other knights also give up the struggle, leaving only Galahad, Bors, and Perceval to carry on the search. All three eventually do find the grail, but only Galahad is allowed to look inside the vessel and fully experience its mysteries.

With the grail in hand, the three successful questers depart for the legendary city of Sarras—variously said to be in the East or in a "spiritual realm"—where they take part in a mystical Mass of the Grail. During this celebration, Christ himself allegedly appears, first as the celebrant, then as a child, and finally, to the amazement of the three knights, as "a naked man whose hands and feet and body were bleeding." The apparition addresses Arthur's men and, in doing so, reveals the key to the quest: "My knights, my sergeants, my loyal sons, you who in this mortal life have become spiritual creatures and who have sought me out so diligently that I can no longer hide myself from your eyes."

The quest accomplished, Galahad is crowned king of Sarras, only to die a happy man one year into his reign. With him goes the grail, as miraculously as it had first appeared to the gathered knights and royals of Camelot. "A great marvel followed immediately on Galahad's death," records the *Queste,* which goes on to say that "the two remaining companions saw quite plainly a hand coming down from heaven, but not the body it belonged to. It proceeded straight to the Holy Vessel and took both it and the lance, and carried them up to heaven." Finally, with Galahad dead and the grail gone, Perceval returns to the Grail Castle, there to rule as king of the newly verdant Waste Land, while Sir Bors, a man as ordinary as Galahad was pure, gallops off to Camelot to tell the tale. And never has there been a man since, declared Malory, who has dared to say he saw the Holy Grail.

Despite the finality of Malory's words, many people since Galahad's day have been bold enough to at least try for such a glimpse. Soldiers and scholars, Crusaders and pilgrims, all variety of seekers have continued to pursue what one modern observer calls this "unimaginably sacred, unimaginably precious" relic. And for at least one doughty Crusader early in the twelfth century, the prize seemed to be securely in hand.

Guglielmo Embriaco was among the many soldiers to seek the grail in the Holy Land. This Italian adventurer's remarkable story embraces in its telling such notable figures as King Solomon, the Queen of Sheba, and even Napoleon. Scion of a powerful Genoese family, Guglielmo sailed to the Middle East in 1099 and took part in the First Crusade. He was among the Europeans who succeeded in capturing Jerusalem that year, and two years later, his Genoese troops helped take the venerable seaport of Tyre. For Guglielmo, the spoils of war included a share of the booty captured in Tyre, specifically the Sacro Catino, or Holy Bowl, which was said to be the Holy Grail. Hexagonal in shape and dark green in color, it was thought to have been carved from a single emerald. Legend also had it that the bowl was a gift to King Solomon from an admiring Queen of Sheba. Only centuries later did it figure in the Last Supper and in the aftermath of the Crucifixion.

Perceval, Galahad, and Bors pray before the grail at the end of their arduous quest. One hundred fifty knights set out to find the vessel, but only three, because of their respective traits of innocence, purity, and humility, succeeded.

Guglielmo brought the captured treasure home to Genoa and installed it in a place of honor in the cathedral of San Lorenzo. There it was revered as a holy relic and as a precious gem, while kings and clerics contested its ownership. At one point in 1522, Spanish troops besieged Genoa, allegedly for no other purpose than to reclaim the precious bowl. Battering rams were brought to bear on the doors of the cathedral, and a pitched battle ensued with the priests inside, but the bowl, hidden behind the heavy wrought-iron gates of the church, was not discovered.

Luck ran out for the Sacro Catino in 1806, however, when the armies of Napoleon marched into Genoa and seized the putative grail. In Paris, the bowl was subjected to a rigorous examination by a special commission of scientists, who declared that whatever its true nature, the bowl had not been carved from a single emerald. Instead, the Sacro Catino was an elaborately cut piece of glass, dating perhaps to the first century. Even worse, by the time the bowl was returned to Genoa, it had been shattered into ten pieces, and the examining committee had appropriated one of the pieces for display in the Louvre.

The intriguing trail of the Crusaders has also led unexpectedly to a recent theory that the grail was neither bowl nor cup, but an ornate little chest. The theory was advanced by historian Noel Currer-Briggs in a 1987 book called *The Shroud and the Grail.* It is his view that the grail was actually a small metal casket used to hold the Shroud of Turin, which he believes is the authentic bloodstained burial cloth of Jesus. This ancient linen, known today by the name of the city in which it has resided for several centuries, bears an image of a crucified man that matches the historical descriptions of Christ.

According to Currer-Briggs, the quest for this incarnation of the Holy Grail began in 1171 when Amalric, the king of Jerusalem, visited his father-in-law, Emperor Manuel I Comnenus of Constantinople. At some point during Amalric's two-month-long stay, the emperor treated his son-in-law to a tour of the palace, showing off even its most secret nooks and sanctuaries. "Nothing was hidden," wrote William, the archbishop of Tyre, who, as Amalric's spiritual adviser, accompanied him on the tour. The family's most prized possessions were all brought forth for inspection. Among the treasures William claimed to have examined were the "most precious evidence of the Passion of Our Lord, namely the cross, nails, lance, sponge, reed, crown of thorns, sindon (that is the cloth in which He was wrapped) and the sandals."

Contending that the holy shroud of the Savior was traditionally stored in the grail, Currer-Briggs assumes that that treasure as well must have been part of Emperor Manuel's trove, even though it seems to have escaped the notice of the archbishop. In any event, word spread that the most sacred relics in all of Christendom were to be found in Constantinople, and great interest and greed were aroused among the knights and nobles of Europe. In 1198, the Fourth Crusade was organized, but this time the objective was Constantinople rather than Jerusalem.

The capital of the Byzantine Empire fell to the Crusaders in 1204 and the city was summarily sacked. The victors helped themselves to whatever treasures they found, even going so far as to cart off the relics of saints from the local churches and cathedrals. Included in the plunder, Currer-Briggs believes, were both the shroud and the grail.

These much-prized items came into the possession of a Frenchman, the Marquis Boniface of Montferrat, and later they were transported to Athens by one of Boniface's closest friends. From this point, Currer-Briggs relies entirely on circumstantial evidence in tracking the passage of the precious cargo through northern Greece, Yugoslavia, and eventually Germany, where it fell into the hands of the Knights Templars. The Templars, Currer-Briggs believes, took the shroud and grail to France by the middle of the thirteenth century, but within a few decades the two great relics had parted company. Currer-Briggs follows the shroud into the keeping of a famed knight, Geoffrey de Charny, and eventually into the custody of the Roman Catholic church. The grail, however, vanishes from sight, evaporating into the world of myth.

In the persistent quest for clues to the grail's present whereabouts, many seekers have reexamined the stories of the vessel's first caretaker, Joseph of Arimathea. As detailed in various grail narratives and their sequels, after the Crucifixion Joseph took custody of Christ's body and laid it in a nearby tomb. The Gospels corroborate this much of the story. The grail narratives add that, in preparing the body for burial, Joseph used the chalice from the Last Supper to catch some of the blood that spilled from Christ's wounds. In doing so, he transformed the cup into one of the most sacred of relics.

Following Christ's Resurrection, Joseph was arrested and accused of having stolen the corpse. Imprisoned and doomed to a slow death by starvation, he withered away to little more than skin and bone until his misery was suddenly brought to an end in a sudden blaze of blinding light. In front of him, as Robert de Borron described the scene, stood the risen Christ bearing "a great and precious vessel." The trembling Joseph was given the Holy Grail and told that anyone who looks upon it will experience lasting joy. Each day thereafter a dove appeared in Joseph's cell and left a single wafer of bread in the cup. He was miraculously sustained by this meager nourishment and survived in prison for the next forty-two years, until he was finally set free by a Roman general named Vespasian, in the year AD 70.

Many of the grail narratives next put the newly freed Joseph adrift on the Mediterranean with neither oars to enable him to catch the tide nor sails to catch the wind. By all accounts he was accompanied by his sister and her husband Bron, and in some of those accounts he brought along a number of other people as well—among them Lazarus, Martha, and Mary Magdalene. Grail theorists have examined minutely the wanderings of this party in hopes of finding clues to the subsequent whereabouts of the treasure.

As legend has it, Joseph made his way around the European continent and eventually washed up on the coast of Britain, a place that some believe might already have been familiar to him: He was supposedly a prosperous tin merchant and, even in those distant times, Britain was known as a source of tin. Indeed, some local Cornish traditions suggest that Joseph not only had visited Britain before but had brought along Jesus and his mother Mary on an earlier trip. Needless to say, such a theory is unprovable.

Once in Britain, Joseph and his companions apparently settled at Glastonbury, a site that would later come to be associated with King Arthur and would be described as "a heavenly sanctuary on earth" by twelfth-century historian William of Malmesbury. There, the travelers allegedly established the first Christian community in Britain. There also, it was said, Joseph died and was buried, with custody of the grail passing to Bron and eventually to Galahad.

How the grail might have moved from Galahad's keeping in Britain back to the vicinity of Antioch and Jerusalem is less clear, although one legend puts the relic into the hands of a group of Crusaders setting out for the Holy Land. It was allegedly their hope to return the grail to the place whence it had originally come. Their plan went awry, however, when they were defeated in battle and decided to abandon the grail, hiding it in the earth for fear that it might fall into enemy hands. Exactly where this might have occurred may never be known.

Another tradition maintains that the grail never left Britain at all, but remains to this day at Glastonbury, where it was either buried or lost. All that can be said with certainty is what archaeology can verify, and that is that the stone ruins at Glastonbury date from the twelfth through the fourteenth centuries. Beneath them lie traces of earlier buildings made of wattle and daub and destroyed by fire in 1184. These modest structures could indeed be the remains of the "Old Church" said to have been constructed there by Joseph of Arimathea in homage to the Virgin Mary.

Nearby, rising 520 feet over the flat landscape of Somerset is Glastonbury Tor, a massive hill associated with the legends of Arthur and said by some to be the burial place of the grail. Nearby, too, is a well filled with spring water that

When this gleaming bronze bowl turned up during an 1893 excavation near Glastonbury, grail seekers hoped their quest had ended. Experts, however, identified the vessel not as the holy chalice but rather as an older, locally made artifact. That led some modern Druids to declare it sacred to their faith and to drink from a replica of it during midsummer ceremonies.

carries red iron oxide leached from the local soil. Traditionally called the Blood Spring for the reddish stains its waters leave, the well is also known by the name Chalice Well, because a legend holds that the grail was once hurled into it, never to be seen again.

Still another tradition suggests that the grail never even reached the British Isles but only got as far as Marseilles, on the southern coast of France. According to this legend, the grail was never in the care of Joseph of Arimathea but was entrusted instead to Mary Magdalene.

At this point, a leap of faith is required to move the grail from Marseilles to the Munsalvaesche of Wolfram von Eschenbach's *Parzifal,* because there is no explanation to be had in the folklore. But there may not have been many miles involved in the transition, since it is widely believed that Wolfram's fictional castle was a guise for the nearby fortress of Montségur in the Languedoc region of France. In any event, the grail is said to have somehow passed from Mary Magdalene to the priests, or Perfecti, of the Cathar sect, who kept it at their stronghold at Montségur. There, they made it a part of a ritual feast called the *manisola.* Eventually, it is said, the Perfecti were forced to hide the cup in one of the many caves that honeycomb the mountain—this, just before the Catholic church finally moved in to close the Montségur monastery, in the process of snuffing out the last vestiges of the heretical sect.

Not surprisingly, places such as Montségur, Glastonbury, and Antioch have attracted a great deal of attention from grail questers over the centuries. In recent years, however, the hardy adventurers traditionally associated with the search have been joined by another variety of seeker, whose specialty might be termed historical detective work. As Sir Thomas Malory's fifteenth-century retelling of the Arthurian saga spread the grail story to an even wider audience than it had before, the book seemed to mark an end to the outpouring of medieval literature on the subject. The next few centuries produced little more than adaptations of earlier works, complete with scholarly commentary. This dearth of fresh ideas and excitement contributed to a growing perception that the grail was nothing more than a Christianized relic of a long-abandoned pagan heritage. By the second half of the twentieth century, however, the new breed of intellectual sleuths was offering theories that revitalized interest in the grail. Some of the modern researchers reassessed the nature of the grail itself, asserting that it was neither a cup nor a platter as the medieval authors had contended.

English author Lady Flavia Anderson fired the first salvo in this process of reevaluation. In 1953 she published a book called *The Ancient Secret,* in which she claimed to have discerned a hidden theme running through the vast majority of legends and folk tales relating to the grail. Lady Flavia believed that the grail was not a cup from the Last Supper, but a water-filled globe that worked like a magnifying lens to turn invisible sunlight into visible flame. Taken at face value, such a peculiar object would hardly seem to fulfill the traditions associated with the grail. According to Lady Flavia, however, just such a globe was the Sacrum, or holy object, of a sun-worshiping cult that had flourished in many parts of the world in the days of the Druids, long before the birth of King Arthur. A branch of this cult had survived in the English town of Glastonbury, she noted, "from the earliest times of which we have any record."

Lady Flavia was convinced that references to the sacred orb are sprinkled through the writings of the old poets whose works had preserved the lore of the grail. She believed, moreover, that her discovery would unlock the "significance and the symbolic meaning of the Blessed Trinity," which she referred to as "the threefold nature of God." For that reason, she claimed, the secret of the globe had long been restricted to a small circle of initiates.

Far more startling than Lady Flavia's perplexing view is the theory advanced by Henry Lincoln, Michael Baigent, and Richard Leigh in their 1982 book, *Holy Blood, Holy Grail.* The conclusions that these three men drew stemmed from a simple curiosity about the remarkable turn of fortune experienced in the late nineteenth century by an impoverished French priest named Saunière, who suddenly became very rich. In the course of their research, the trio blew the dust off many old grail texts and followed a trail of clues that led back in time to the birth of Christianity. What they found, they assert, was an ungodly secret and a massive effort by the Roman Catholic church to keep certain facts unknown.

According to Lincoln and his colleagues, Saunière was restoring his village church in 1891 when he stumbled on four ancient parchments concealed underneath the altar stone. Two of the parchments—with letters of uneven sizes and words run together or unnecessarily broken and continued on the line below—gave every indication of being coded messages. Saunière brought the documents to the attention of his superiors and, soon afterward, was observed to be spending large sums of money that were clearly beyond his means. The authors contend his sudden wealth was paid out by Church authorities in Rome in exchange for continued silence on the matter of the parchments. The documents allegedly revealed that the Crucifixion had never transpired and that Christ had lived on to wed Mary Magdalene, with whom he had fathered at least one child. The parchments also proved—or so the writers claimed—that descendants of Jesus were probably still alive today.

Measuring nearly sixteen inches in diameter and three and a half in height, the green glass Sacro Catino, or Holy Bowl, maintains a mesmerizing allure despite permanent scars from scientists' brutal—and unsuccessful—attempts to confirm it as the grail.

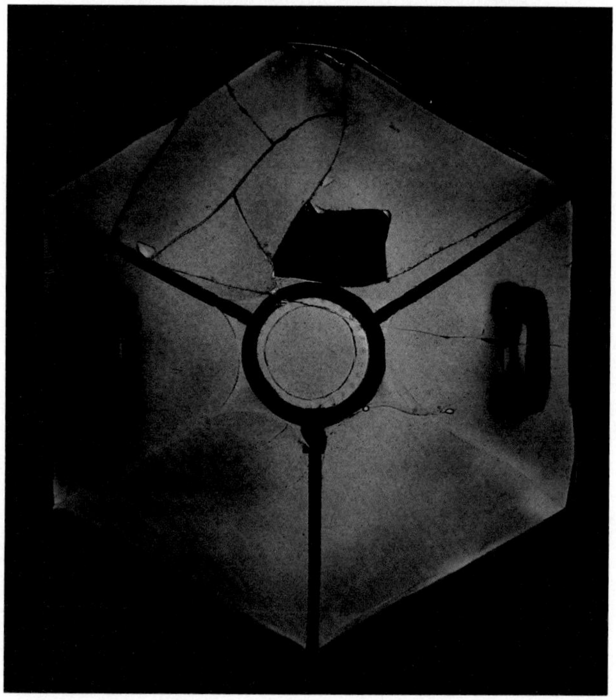

As Lincoln, Baigent, and Leigh would have it, this astonishing secret was preserved for many centuries because of a drastic misconception about two important words: The Holy Grail should not have been the *Saint Graal* or *Saint Gréal* that has always been depicted in legend. It should have been the *Sang Réal* or "royal blood" of Jesus that has been carried by his heirs down through the generations. From this bloodline, the theory contends, came the Merovingian dynasty of European kings, who ruled what is now southern France during the early Middle Ages. This lineage was brought to an end by the assassination of Dagobert II in AD 679—a murder that was committed, the authors suggest, by a conspiratorial group of high church officials.

In support of this highly speculative argument, the theorists point to Wolfram von Eschenbach's insistence that Arthur's court was located not in Britain but in France. They also suggest that the predecessors of the Knights Templars, who were historically regarded as the keepers of the Holy Grail, were actually the protectors of the Merovingian dynasty. Their the-

Joseph of Arimathea—who according to legend transported the grail to England—bows his haloed head in homage to the sacred chalice in this modern painting. From his right arm hangs the death shroud he purchased for the slain Christ.

The mysterious priest-king Prester John blesses his realm in this fifteenth-century German woodcut. According to the Latin inscription, he ruled India and Ethiopia. Some sources reckon his worldly holdings to have included the grail, claiming he inherited it from his uncle, the hero Perceval.

ory, say Lincoln and his colleagues, also makes sense of the enigmatic character of the Fisher King, a fixture in most grail lore. The king who cannot die but is powerless to rule signifies the descendants of Jesus Christ, who are effectively crippled by the secret they are required to maintain. Not many historians have found merit in this unconventional view of the past.

If purity of heart is a prerequisite to success in finding the Holy Grail, as the writings of Robert de Borron seem to show, then it has been left to the twentieth century to provide the least likely quester of all. In the 1920s, Adolf Hitler declared: "I am founding an Order. It is from there that the second stage will emerge—the stage of the Man-God." His crusade was for nothing less than world domination, and his elite Order was the fearsome Schutzstaffel, or "Security Service," more familiarly known as the SS.

In its command structure, secret oaths, and rituals, the SS was fashioned after the knightly religious brotherhoods of medieval Germany. Its members were set apart by their dramatic black uniforms, replete with silver insignia. The men of the new Black Order answered to Hitler's confidant, Heinrich Himmler, among whose more benign interests was the study of Wolfram von Eschenbach's *Parzifal.* The SS chief's dabblings in esoteric matters also led him to an interest in the Cathars, and he found in one of the teachings of that sect—its preoccupation with the conflict between the forces of darkness and light—additional justification for the frenzied Nazi hatred of Jews. Himmler and other high Nazi officials came to think of the cause of the National Socialists as a battle of the righteous, light-skinned Aryans against the destructive influences of the dark-skinned Semites.

Heinrich Himmler envisioned his SS as the natural heirs to the Holy Grail, and he believed that once his party had captured this prize, it could rightly claim to rule the world. He saw confirmation for this belief in the scholarship of Otto Rahn, a medievalist who had made a study of the lost cultures of Provence and Languedoc. Rahn, who had lately become an officer in the SS, read great significance into the passages from *Parzifal* in which Wolfram describes the sources of his work: "Guyot, the master of high renown, / Found in confused pagan writing, / The legend which reaches back to the prime source of all legends." These lines, Rahn believed, proved that the grail was not a cup but a set of stone or wooden tablets on which the sum of all esoteric knowledge had been inscribed, probably in runic characters. Himmler and at least a few of his colleagues came to believe that the tablets might prove to be the long-lost Book of the Aryans—a pagan "Ten Commandments," which would support their notion of an Aryan superrace.

Like many others before him, Rahn regarded Wolfram's Munsalvaesche to be one and the same with the real-world Montségur, in Languedoc. His conviction that the Cathars had possessed the grail seemed to be bolstered by old church documents he had read that recorded the final onslaught at Montségur, during the campaign to stamp out Catharism. Among other things, these papers related the story of four Cathars who escaped the mountain stronghold by lowering themselves down the cliff that surrounded it on ropes and then made off with the grail. Local tradition had it that they stashed the precious booty in a cave in the nearby mountains.

Accordingly, in 1931 Himmler ordered Rahn to rummage through the ruins of Montségur and, if possible, to bring the grail home to Germany. Rahn proceeded to the south of France, and donning the guise of an archaeologically minded tourist on holiday, endeavored to carry out this order. A chance encounter with an old shepherd, early in his stay, convinced Rahn that he was on the right track. The old man, repeating a local legend in which the pope is equated with the devil, told Rahn that "during the time when the walls of Montségur were still standing, the Cathars kept the Holy Grail there. Montségur was in danger, the armies of Lucifer had besieged it. They wanted the grail, to restore it to their Prince's diadem from which it had fallen during the fall of the angels." But before that could happen, the shepherd went on, the "keeper of the Grail threw the sacred jewel into the depths of the mountain. The mountain closed up again, and in this manner was the Grail saved. When the devils entered the fortress, they were too late."

Otto Rahn spent three months searching in and around Montségur, apparently without success. Nevertheless, he was promoted to colonel for his efforts, and he went on to describe his theories on the end of Catharism in a book called *Crusade Against the Grail,* published in 1933. In the pressing business of organizing Hitler's so-called Thousand-Year Reich, the SS did not send Rahn back to Montségur until 1937. By that time, Himmler had grown so certain of Rahn's eventual success that he was already planning an elaborate sanctuary for the grail.

Twenty-seven-year-old Otto Rahn, a grail scholar commissioned by the Nazis to unearth the holy relic, searches a graffiti-marked cave on Montségur in France.

No one today can say with certainty whether or not the grail was ever captured by Nazis. It is known that Otto Rahn committed suicide after returning from Montségur for the second time, and he took to the grave whatever secrets he knew. Since that time, death has silenced most of the other participants in this little-known chapter of Nazi history. It has been suggested that Rahn's suicide proves that he did indeed find what he was looking for, and that he could not live with the awful knowledge it had revealed. Some who have studied the subject believe that several years later, when Nazi successes on the battlefields of World War II put France under German occupation, the SS returned to Montségur to claim Rahn's grail and to carry it back to Germany. There is evidence that such a mission may have been carried out in 1943 or early 1944. If so, the grail has since vanished, apparently without a trace.

Century after century, the search for the Holy Grail goes on. For some, the quest becomes a pilgrimage of the soul, part of a lifelong crusade to transform themselves—as Galahad, Perceval, and Bors did—into "spiritual creatures" capable of overcoming any adversity to uncover the grail within. For others, the quest is more material; it is a chance to follow in the footsteps of those who quested before, in the enduring hope of bringing to hand what others failed to find. Every year, some 150,000 people make the pilgrimage to Glastonbury, England, one of the legendary resting places of the Holy Grail. Among those many thousands, as they stoop over the Chalice Well and peer into its reddish-staining waters, not a few surely feel the unmistakable nearness of mystery.

Perched atop the peak of Montségur, this ruined Cathar temple allegedly concealed the grail within some hidden sacred niche.

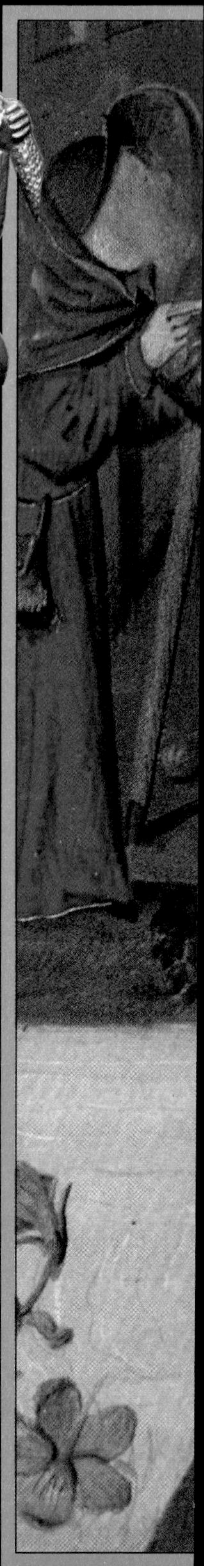

The Pursuit of the Sorcerer

As mentor and ally to King Arthur, the redoubtable sorcerer Merlin has fascinated Westerners for more than a thousand years. England, Scotland, and Wales, in particular, are awash in tales of his marvelous life. He is said to have learned to speak fluently by eighteen months of age and to have called forth clear-eyed visions of the future throughout his days. The spirit of this storied character is oddly real for many admirers, who sense his presence in special places such as Tintagel Castle in Cornwall, where he is said to have plotted Arthur's conception, and in the environs of Stonehenge where—some believe—he personally arrayed the great stone circle. Since the Middle Ages when minstrels began spreading word of his exploits, the legends of Merlin have steadily compounded. In the process, the historical figure who inspired the stories—if there ever was such a person—has grown increasingly difficult to know. Among the historians who have sought to dissolve the patina of embellishment, writer Nikolai Tolstoy, for one, believes that he has succeeded.

Enthralled since childhood by Arthurian tales in the works of Malory and Tennyson, Tolstoy decided in the early 1980s to search for the real Merlin. As recounted in his book, *The Quest for Merlin,* his hunt led from dusty tomes in medieval libraries to the Scottish Lowlands where the fabled sorcerer may have lived and worked. Tolstoy concluded that the historical Merlin was a far cry from the wizard of Camelot: No mere attendant to the Christian Arthur, he was a stalwart Celt, a pagan priest, a mystic, and a hermit.

British-born Count Nikolai Tolstoy (left), whose famous Russian forebear Leo Tolstoy wrote War and Peace, works amid a collection of Celtic texts at his farmhouse near Oxford. Tolstoy believes the Celts revered Merlin as an embodiment of the stag god, whose image—from an old Celtic bowl called the Gundestrup cauldron—appears here and on the following pages.

Young Merlin is depicted in the painting below hooded in blue and uttering his first prophecy. The precocious lad had been summoned by King Vortigern of Britain to be offered as a human sacrifice, but he saved himself by revealing the presence of dragons under the castle foundations. Merlin saw the monsters as a portent of war between the Britons and Saxons.

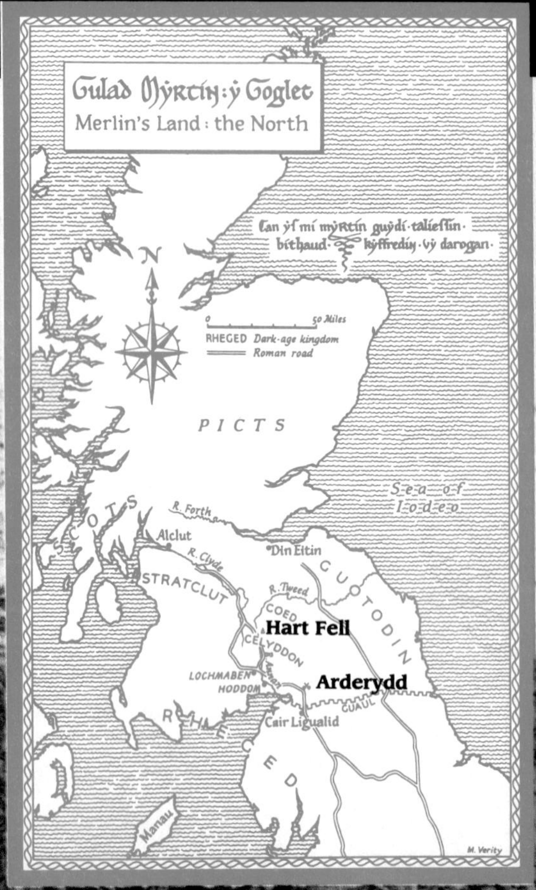

Tolstoy visits the Moat of Liddel, where Merlin may have fought in the Battle of Arderydd. The fortifications occupy a strategic high ground vital to any

ny crossing between the northwest of England and the Scottish Lowlands.

A Magical Bard on the Battlefield

In search of the legend's roots, Tolstoy perused the earliest writings on Merlin. He found the soundest information in the works of a twelfth-century British historian, Geoffrey of Monmouth, and in a collection of Welsh poetry anthologized in the 1400s.

Geoffrey's initial portrayal of Merlin had helped to popularize the characterization of a wise and powerful guardian to Arthur. But a later volume, *The Life of Merlin,* told a different story and painted a newly revealing portrait—one that was borne out by descriptions in the Welsh poetry. In both sources Merlin was depicted as a bard in the court of a pagan Scottish king.

Fascinated by this view, Tolstoy expanded the scope of his detective work. He sought the locations described by Geoffrey, first on maps and later in the hills and glens of Scotland. Encouraged by substantiating clues in the Welsh poetry, he traced the bard's movements to a place once known as Arderydd on the English-Scottish border *(map, opposite).* In AD 573, the forces of the Celtic king Gwenddolau assembled in this region to meet the armies of Rhydderch, a champion of Christianity. As Gwenddolau's bard, Merlin took part in the battle.

Gwenddolau was killed in the fighting, and his army was destroyed. As for Merlin, Geoffrey reports: "A strange madness came upon him. He crept away and fled to the woods, unwilling that any should see his going. For a whole summer he stayed hidden in the woods, discovered by none, forgetful of himself and of his own."

Nikolai Tolstoy rests for a moment at Hartfell Spa, which he believes to be Merlin's grotto. "One of the holiest places in Britain," he called it, remembering that "one magical April day I found myself stooping to drink from that enchanted spring by which the wizard uttered his wild mantic strains." The pool's rusty-tasting waters, which are heavily laden with iron salts, snake through the hills below the peak of Hart Fell, which rises a commanding 2,652 feet above sea level. In England and Scotland, the word fell denotes a highland plateau. This one was probably given the name Hart because herds of deer—or harts—once grazed on its slopes. As Tolstoy has noted, Merlin came to be identified with the horned animals, and this probably led to an identification with the stag deity.

Mad Merlin's Wild and Lonely Place

In the aftermath of Arderydd, Merlin reportedly roamed the forests half-mad and overcome with grief. His wanderings took him to what Geoffrey described as "a spring on the very top of a certain mountain." Tolstoy set out to find this retreat.

Literary sources pointed to a woodland that held several likely sites, but Tolstoy had a medieval romance called *Fergus* to help narrow the field. The book referred to a place "where Merlin dwelt many a year," and it was considered generally reliable in its geographical descriptions. It led to a mountain called Hart Fell (*below*), where Tolstoy found a spring with waters that were unusually chalybeate—that is, high in iron content. By a roundabout logic Tolstoy discovered that this quality of the water provided an important clue.

He recalled Geoffrey's reference to Merlin's retreat "in the country of Gewisse at the Fountain of Galabes," and he reasoned that the name Galabes may well have been a simplified spelling of *calabeatus,* Latin for chalybeate. He noted, moreover, that Gewisse was an early name for the region around Hart Fell.

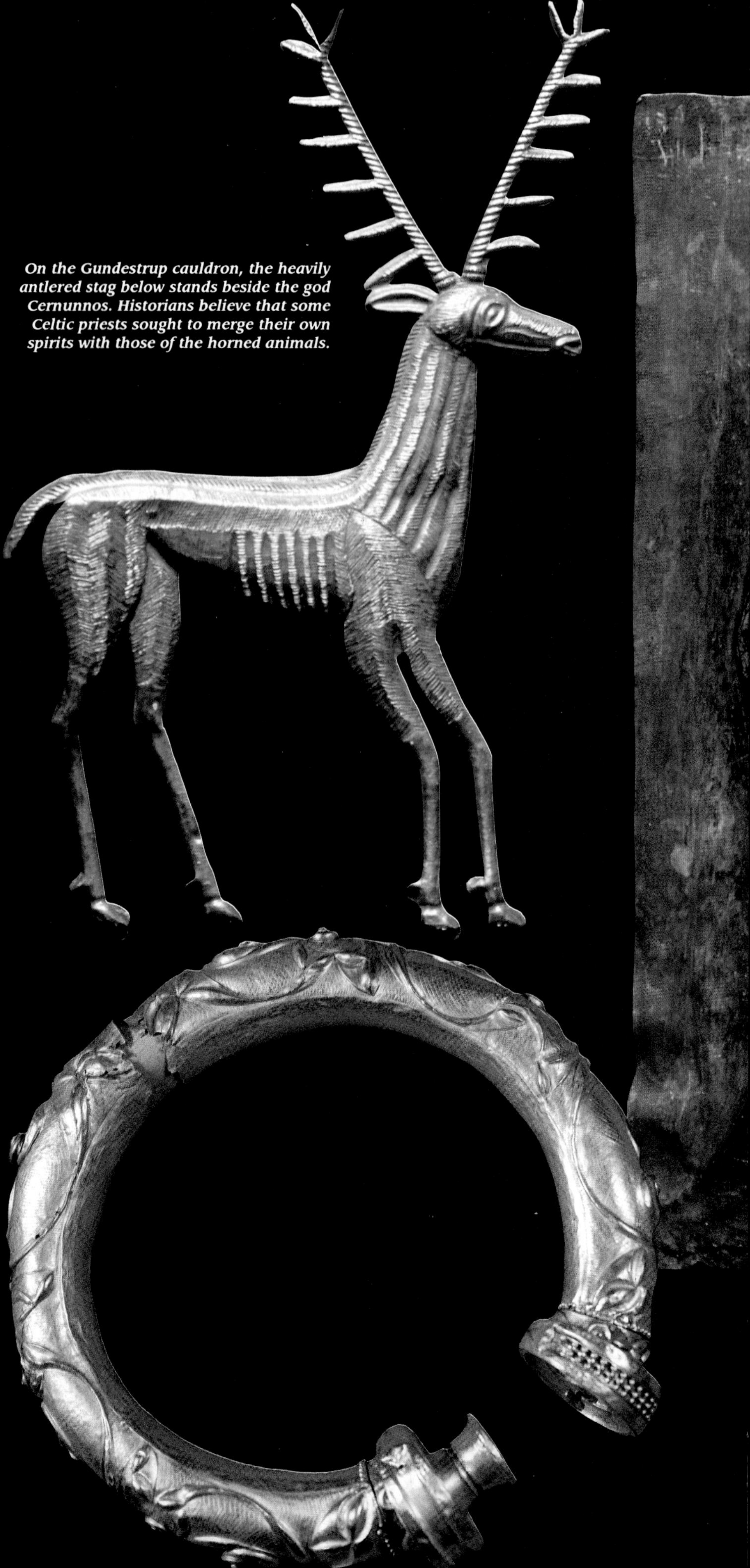

On the Gundestrup cauldron, the heavily antlered stag below stands beside the god Cernunnos. Historians believe that some Celtic priests sought to merge their own spirits with those of the horned animals.

Lord of the Animals

In his hermitage on Hart Fell, Tolstoy asserts, Merlin came to be greatly revered by the local Celts. The horned god with whom he would have been identified was the one sometimes called Cernunnos. Like the figure above from the Gundestrup cauldron, Cernunnos was often depicted as a man with a stag's ears and antlers. The deity was worshiped as a denizen of the wilderness who wielded power over the forest animals and felt a strong affinity for them. Stags, in particular, were at his beck and call, but he also commanded boars and wolves.

Naturally, one of Cernunnos's titles was Lord of the Animals, and Merlin's association with this god probably sprang from his many years among the wild creatures. Geoffrey of Monmouth wrote that Merlin adopted an aged wolf as his companion, and the Welsh poets told how he rendered his prophecies with the aid of a pig. As with Cernunnos, however, Merlin's chief forest ally was probably the stag.

Geoffrey recorded that the bard-turned-hermit once returned to his long-abandoned wife and raged against her plans to remarry. Storming into the wedding astride a great stag, he hurled antlers at the bridegroom and wound up "knocking him lifeless."

Tolstoy shares the view of other scholars that Merlin may have been a Druid—a priest and prophet of the Celtic religion. Although the Romans had tried to eliminate this faith during their tenure in Britain, a few strongholds probably survived and Merlin could have become a respected elder.

In another portrait from the Gundestrup cauldron, a bearded deity hoists a buck in each hand, revealing his identity as the stag god with whom Tolstoy links Merlin. The figure flaunts his supremacy over the animals by displaying the ease with which he overpowers them.

n ancient Celtic emblem of power (left), this old Irish torque from the first century BC is ecorated with leaves, spirals, and trumpets. uch a collar, says one Welsh poem, adorned Ierlin's neck at the Battle of Arderydd.

ACKNOWLEDGMENTS

The editors wish to thank the following individuals and institutions for their valuable assistance in the preparation of this volume:
Professor Emmanuel Anati, Capo di Ponte, Brescia, Italy; Carol Andrews, British Museum, London; Christian Balister, Chef du Service Photo, Bibliothèque Royale Albert Ier, Brussels; P. Leonard E. Boyle, O. P., the Prefect, Biblioteca Apostolica Vaticana, Rome; Marco Carrieri, Milan, Italy; Richard Erdoes, Santa Fe, New Mexico; Albano Guatti, Udine, Italy; Heidi Klein, Bildarchiv Preussischer Kulturbesitz, Berlin; Atila Koc, Governor, Siir Province, Turkey; Archie P. Lame Deer, Sturgess, South Dakota; Paola Lazard, Paris; Christopher Rawlings, British Library, London; C. S. Reid, Kenora, Ontario, Canada; Stephan A. Schwartz, The Mobius Society, Los Angeles, California; Peter Stocks, British Library, London; Christiane Van Den Bergen, Attachée à la Section des Manuscrits, Bibliothèque Royale Albert Ier, Brussels.

PICTURE CREDITS

The sources for the illustrations in this book are listed below. Credits for illustrations shown from left to right are separated by semicolons; credits from top to bottom are separated by dashes.
Cover: Art by Bryan Leister. 6-17: Art by John Collier. 19: Comstock Inc./Michael Stuckey. 20: Courtesy the Nicholas Roerich Museum, New York—UPI/Bettmann, New York. 21: Culver Pictures, Inc., New York. 24: Réunion des Musées Nationaux, Paris. 25, 26: From *The Way to Shambhala,* by Edwin Bernbaum, Doubleday, Garden City, N.Y., 1980. 28, 29: Lee Boltin, Croton-on-Hudson, New York; courtesy the Trustees of the British Library, London (2). 33: Michael Holford, London. 34: Bildarchiv Preussischer Kulturbesitz, Berlin. 35: Michael Holford, London. 36, 37: Bildarchiv Preussischer Kulturbesitz, Berlin; Verlag Philipp von Zabern, Mainz/Jürgen Liepe; Luisa Ricciarini, Milan. 38: Saint Augustine Historical Society, Saint Augustine, Fla. 42: Roger Weld, © 1991/Andean Explorers Foundation and Ocean Sailing Club, Reno, Nev.—Dale Wittner/Andean Explorers Foundation and Ocean Sailing Club, Reno, Nev. 44, 45: Prof. Emmanuel Anati, Capo di Ponte, Brescia, Italy. 46, 47: Biblioteca Apostolica Vaticana, Rome. 48: David Rubinger/*Time* magazine. 49: Nationalmuseet, Copenhagen, Denmark; map by Fred Holz; Tim Severin/photo by Nazeum Chouleh. 50, 51: Map by Fred Holz; © Kevin Fleming, Annapolis, Md. 52, 53: © Kevin Fleming, Annapolis, Md. (2); map by Fred Holz—Badisches Landesmuseum Karlsruhe. 54, 55: © Kevin Fleming, Annapolis, Md. (2)—map by Fred Holz—Scala, Florence, courtesy Biblioteca Apostolica Vaticana, Rome. 56, 57: Map by Fred Holz; The Metropolitan Museum of Art, gift of Amelia E. White, 1941—Sotheby's, London; Tim Severin/photo by Kevin Fleming. 58, 59: Tim Severin/photo by Kevin Fleming; Michael Holford, London—© Kevin Fleming, Annapolis, Md.; map by Fred Holz. 60: Tim Severin/photo by Kevin Fleming. 61: Tim Severin/photo by Kevin Fleming—Réunion des Musées Nationaux, Paris. 63: Scala, Florence. 65: Yücel Donmez, courtesy the High Flight Foundation, Colorado Springs. 66: NASA. 67: Map by Fred Holz. 68, 69: Robert Harding Picture Library, London. 72: Bibliothèque Nationale, Paris—Scala, Florence, courtesy SS. Marcellino and Pietro, Rome; Israel Museum, Jerusalem. 73: Courtesy the Trustees of the British Library, London. 74: Courtesy Lloyd Bailey, Duke University Divinity School, Durham, N.C. 75: Courtesy the Trustees of the British Museum, London. 77: From *Kapoot,* by Carveth Wells, Jarrold Publishers, London, 1934. 78: Marka, Milan; Scala, Florence, courtesy the Musei Vaticani, Rome. 80: Mary Evans Picture Library, London—courtesy the Trustees of the British Museum, London. 81: Mary Evans Picture Library, London. 82: Scala, Florence. 85-87: Fernand Navarra, Bordeaux. 90: Turkish Army Mapping Service. 91-94: David Fasold, Poway, Calif. 95: Bureau of American Ethnology, Bulletin 19, "An Introduction to the Tres Zapotes Veracruz, Mexico," by Clarence W. Weiant. 96, 97: Courtesy Marion Stirling Pugh; Matthew W. Stirling, © National Geographic Society—Clarence Weiant, courtesy Stephan A. Schwartz; Richard H. Stewart, © National Geographic Society (2); Bureau of American Ethnology, Bulletin 19, "An Introduction to the Tres Zapotes Veracruz, Mexico," by Clarence W. Weiant. 98: The Mobius Society, Los Angeles. 99: Courtesy Stephan A. Schwartz (2)—reproduced with the permission of the Ontario Ministry of Culture and Communications. 100: George Brich—© 1985 The Mobius Society, Los Angeles (2). 101-103: © 1985 The Mobius Society, Los Angeles. 104, 105: The *Times,* London. 107: National Museum of Ireland, Dublin. 108, 109: Holy Shroud Guild/photo by G. Enrie. 110: Courtesy the Trustees of the British Library, London. 112, 113: Janet and Colin Bord, Clwyd, Wales; Simon McBride/Susan Griggs, London. 114: Photo by Roloff Beny/National Archives of Canada. 115: Museum für Islamische Kunst, Staatliche Museen Preussischer Kulturbesitz, Berlin/photo by Stüning. 116: Leonard Sleath/The Chalice Well Trust, Glastonbury, Somerset, England—Janet and Colin Bord, Clwyd, Wales. 119: Bibliothèque Nationale, Paris. 120: Bibliothèque Royale Albert Ier, Brussels. 121: Bibliothèque Nationale, Paris. 124: Somerset County Museum, Taunton, Somerset, England. 125: Mario Carrieri, Milan. 126: From *The Grail,* by John Matthews, © 1981 Thames and Hudson Ltd., London. 127: Giuliano Dati, *Treatise on the Supreme Prester John* (published 1495). 128: Jean-Loup Charmet, Paris/Courtesy Editions Robert Laffont. 129: Jean Dieuzaide, Toulouse, France. 130, 131: Roy Cook, Hampton Hill, Middlesex, England; Nationalmuseet, Copenhagen, Denmark; Lambeth Palace Library, London. 132, 133: Map by N. Tolstoy; N. Tolstoy/photo by Michael Florence; Nationalmuseet, Copenhagen, Denmark. 134, 135: N. Tolstoy, except top right Nationalmuseet, Copenhagen, Denmark. 136, 137: Nationalmuseet, Copenhagen, Denmark, except bottom left National Museum of Ireland, Dublin.

BIBLIOGRAPHY

Achtemeier, Paul J., ed., *Harper's Bible Dictionary.* San Francisco: Harper & Row, 1985.
Anati, Emmanuel:
"Has Mt. Sinai Been Found?" *Biblical Archaeology Review,* July-August 1985.
The Mountain of God: Har Karkom. Transl. by Montagna di Dio. New York: Rizzoli, 1986.
Anderson, Flavia, *The Ancient Secret: In Search of the Holy Grail.* London: Victor Gollancz, 1953.
Angebert, Jean-Michel, *The Occult and the Third Reich: The Mystical Origins of Nazism and the Search for the Holy Grail.* Transl. by Lewis A. M. Sumberg. New York: Macmillan, 1974.
Asimov, Isaac, *Asimov's Guide to the Bible, Volume 1: The Old Testament.* Garden City, N.Y.: Doubleday, 1968.
Baigent, Michael, Richard Leigh, and Henry Lincoln, *Holy Blood, Holy Grail.* New York: Delacorte Press, 1982.
Bailey, Lloyd R.:
Noah: The Person and the Story in History and Tradition. Columbia: University of South Carolina Press, 1989.
Where Is Noah's Ark? Nashville: Abingdon, 1978.
Bailey, Richard N., Eric Cambridge, and H. Denis Briggs, *Dowsing and Church Archaeology.* Wimborne, England: Intercept, 1988.
Balsiger, David, and Charles Sellier, Jr., *In Search of Noah's Ark.* Los Angeles: Sun Classic Books, 1976.
Baney, Ralph E., *Search for Sodom and Gomorrah* (2d ed.). Kansas City, Mo.: CAM Press, 1962.
Baumgardner, John R., and M. Salih Bayraktutan, "July 1987 Geophysical Investigation of Noah's Ark (Durupinar Site): Mahser Village, Doğubayazit, Agri." Report. Erzurum, Turkey, November 1987.
Begg, Paul, "The Quest for the Holy Grail." *The Unexplained* (London), Vol. 6, Issue 66.
Berkowitz, Lois, "Has the U.S. Geological Survey Found King Solomon's Gold Mines?" *The Biblical Archaeology Review,* September 1977.
Berlitz, Charles, *The Lost Ship of Noah: In Search of the Ark at Ararat.* New York: G. P. Putnam's Sons, 1987.
Bernbaum, Edwin, *The Way to Shambhala.* Garden City, N.Y.: Doubleday, 1980.
Birks, Walter, and R. A. Gilbert, *The Treasure of Montségur: A Study of the Cathar Heresy and the Nature of the Cathar Secret.* Wellingborough, England: Aquarian Press, 1987.
Black Elk, *The Sacred Pipe.* Ed. by Joseph Epes Brown, Norman: University of Oklahoma Press, 1970.
The Book of Beginnings (The Enchanted World series). Alexandria, Va.: Time-Life Books, 1986.
Bord, Janet, and Colin Bord, *Sacred Waters.* London: Granada, 1985.
Bright, Richard C., *The Ark, A Reality?* Guilderland, N.Y.: Ranger Associates, 1989.
Brinton, Daniel G., *Notes on the Floridian Peninsula: Its Literary History, Indian Tribes and Antiquities.* Philadelphia: Joseph Sabin, 1859.
Bryce, James:
"On Armenia and Mount Ararat." *Proceedings of the Roy-*

al Geographical Society, May 9, 1878.
Transcaucasia and Ararat: Being Notes of a Vacation Tour in the Autumn of 1876. London: Macmillan, 1896.
Bulfinch, Thomas:
Bulfinch's Mythology. New York: Thomas Y. Crowell, 1970.
Myths of Greece and Rome. Comp. by Bryan Holme. Harmondsworth, England: Penquin Books, 1981.
Cavendish, Richard, ed., *Man, Myth & Magic: The Illustrated Encyclopedia of Mythology, Religion and the Unknown* (11 vols.). Freeport, N.Y.: Marshall Cavendish, 1983.
Ceram, C. W., *Gods, Graves, and Scholars* (2d ed.). Transl. by E. B. Garside and Sophie Wilkins. New York: Alfred A. Knopf, 1968.
Chadwick, John, *The Mycenaean World.* Cambridge: Cambridge University Press, 1976.
Clark, Champ, and the Editors of Time-Life Books, *Flood* (Planet Earth series). Alexandria, Va.: Time-Life Books, 1982.
Clarkson, Atelia, and Gilbert B. Cross, *World Folktales: A Scribner Resource Collection.* New York: Charles Scribner's Sons, 1980.
Currer-Briggs, Noel, *The Shroud and the Grail: A Modern Quest for the True Grail.* New York: St. Martin's Press, 1987.
Delaney, Frank, *The Celts.* London: Hodder and Stoughton, 1986.
The Dictionary of Bible and Religion. Nashville: Abingdon Press, 1986.
Di Nola, Alfonso M., "The Secrets of the Ark." *ULISSE 2000* (Rome), April 1991.
Dobbs, Rose, *More Once-Upon A-Time Stories.* New York: Random House, 1961.
Eban, Abba Solomon, *Heritage: Civilization and the Jews.* New York: Simon & Schuster, 1984.
Edwords, Frederick:
"New Evidence for Noah's Ark?" *The Humanist,* November-December 1984.
"Searching for Noah's Ark." *The Humanist,* November-December 1983.
Eliade, Mircea, *A History of Religious Ideas* (Vol. 1). Chicago: University of Chicago Press, 1978.
Eliade, Mircea, ed., *The Encyclopedia of Religion* (Vol. 14). New York: Macmillan, 1987.
Encyclopaedia Judaica. Jerusalem: Keter, 1971.
Erdoes, Richard, *Crying for a Dream: The World through Native American Eyes.* Santa Fe, N.Mex.: Bear, 1990.
Errico, Charles J., and J. Samuel Walker. "The New Deal and the Guru." *American Heritage,* March 1989.
Fasold, David, *The Ark of Noah.* New York: Wynwood, 1989.
Fire, John/Lame Deer, and Richard Erdoes, *Lame Deer: Seeker of Visions.* New York: Simon & Schuster, 1972.
Garlake, Peter, *The Kingdoms of Africa.* Oxford: Elsevier-Phaidon, 1978.
Gaskill, Gordon, "The Mystery of Noah's Ark." *Reader's Digest,* September 1975.
Gaster, Theodor H., *Myth, Legend, and Custom in the Old Testament.* New York: Harper & Row, 1969.
Gorman, James, "Righteous Stuff." *Omni,* May 1984.
The Harper Atlas of the Bible. San Francisco: Harper & Row, 1987.
Harpers Bible Dictionary. San Francisco: Harper & Row, 1985.
"Have Sodom and Gomorrah Been Found?" *Biblical Archaeology Review,* September-October 1980.
Hemming, John, *The Search for El Dorado.* New York: E. P. Dutton, 1979.
Hitching, Francis, *The Mysterious World: An Atlas of the Unexplained.* New York: Holt, Rinehart and Winston, 1979.
The Holy Bible (Authorized King James Version). Cleveland: William Collins & World, no date.
Hoppe, Leslie J., *What Are They Saying about Biblical Archaeology?* New York: Paulist Press, 1984.
Horn, Jeanne, *Hidden Treasure.* New York: Arco, 1962.
Howard-Gordon, Frances, *Glastonbury: Maker of Myths.* Glastonbury, England: Gothic Image, 1982.
Hoxie, Frederick E., *The Crow.* New York: Chelsea House, 1989.
The Interpreter's Dictionary of the Bible (4 vols.). Nashville: Abingdon Press, 1962.
Irwin, James B., "High Flight Expedition: The Search for Noah's Ark." Report. Colorado Springs: High Flight Foundation, 1982.
Irwin, James B., and Monte Unger, *More than an Ark on Ararat.* Nashville: Broadman Press, 1985.
Jackson, Samuel Macauley, ed., *The New Schaff-Herzog Encyclopedia of Religious Knowledge.* Grand Rapids: Baker Book House, 1969.
Jahner, Elaine, "The Spiritual Landscape." *Parabola,* Vol. 2, No. 3, 1989.
The Jewish Encyclopedia (12 vols.). New York: Funk & Wagnalls, 1916.
Keller, Werner, *The Bible as History* (2d rev. ed.). Transl. by William Neil and B. H. Rasmussen. New York: William Morrow, 1981.
Kenyon, Kathleen M., *Archaeology in the Holy Land.* New York: Frederick A. Praeger, 1960.
"King Solomon's Mines in Peru?" *Treasure,* April 1990.
Knipe, Rita, *The Water of Life: A Jungian Journey through Hawaiian Myth.* Honolulu: University of Hawaii Press, 1989.
Kruta, Venceslas, *The Celts of the West.* Transl. by Alan Sheridan. London: Orbis, 1985.
Lacy, Norris J., and Geoffrey Ashe, *The Arthurian Handbook.* New York: Garland, 1988.
Leach, Maria:
How the People Sang the Mountains Up. New York: Viking Press, 1967.
The Lion Sneezed: Folktales and Myths of the Cat. New York: Thomas Y. Crowell, 1977.
Leach, Maria, ed., *Funk & Wagnalls Standard Dictionary of Folklore, Mythology and Legend* (Vol. 2). New York: Funk & Wagnalls, 1949.
MacCana, Proinsias, *Celtic Mythology.* New York: Peter Bedrick Books, 1983.
Mackay, Charles, *Extraordinary Popular Delusions and the Madness of Crowds.* New York: Farrar, Straus and Giroux, 1932 (reprint of 1841 edition).
Mann, Florian A., *The Story of Ponce DeLeon.* Florian A. Mann, 1903.
Marsa, Linda, and Susan M. Silver, "Mobius." *US,* April 13, 1982.
Matarasso, P. M., trans., *The Quest of the Holy Grail.* New York: Penguin Books, 1982.
Matthews, John, *The Grail: Quest for the Eternal.* New York: Crossroad, 1981.
Mazar, Amihai, *Archaeology of the Land of the Bible: 10,000-586 B.C.E.* New York: Doubleday, 1990.
Meshorer, Yaakov, "An Ancient Coin Depicts Noah's Ark." *Biblical Archaeology Review,* September-October 1981.
Millard, Alan, *Treasures from Bible Times.* Belleville, Mich.: Lion, 1985.
Montgomery, John Warwick, *The Quest for Noah's Ark.* Minneapolis: Bethany Fellowship, 1972.
Moore, Robert A. Review of *Where Is Noah's Ark?* by Lloyd R. Bailey. *The Skeptical Inquirer,* Summer 1979.
Myers, Bernard S., ed., *Dictionary of Art* (Vol. 5). London: McGraw-Hill, 1969.
Mysterious Lands and Peoples (Mysteries of the Unknown series). Alexandria, Va.: Time-Life Books, 1991.
Nelson's Illustrated Bible Dictionary. Nashville: Thomas Nelson, 1986.
Nevin, Charles, "The Past and the Paranormal." *The Times Saturday Review (London Times),* October 6, 1990.
New Catholic Encyclopedia. Washington, D.C.: Catholic University of America, 1967.
The New Encyclopaedia Britannica (Micropaedia vols. 1 and 4). Chicago: Encyclopaedia Britannica, 1985.
The New Grolier Atlas of the World. Danbury, Conn.: Grolier, 1988.
Ober, Frederick A., *Juan Ponce de Leon.* New York: Harper & Brothers, 1908.
Ohlendorf, Pat, "Noah's Ark and Biblical Truth." *Maclean's,* October 25, 1982.
Parrish, Michael, "Psychic Raiders of the Lost Arks." *Los Angeles,* August 1984.
Phillis, Michael:
"Explorer of Lost Civilization Returns to Reno." *Reno Gazette-Journal,* December 8, 1987.
"Reno's Version of Indiana Jones Hits Paydirt." *Reno Gazette-Journal,* December 7, 1989.
Regniers, Beatrice Schenk de, *The Giant Book.* New York: Atheneum, 1966.
Reid, C. S., "The Boys Site and the Early Ontario Iroquois Tradition." Archaeological Survey of Canada Paper No. 42. Ottawa, Ontario: National Museums of Canada, 1975.
Roerich, Nicholas, *Heart of Asia.* New York: Roerich Museum Press, 1929.
Rosenfeld, Richard, *Lost Treasures of the World.* Secaucus, N.J.: Chartwell Books, 1986.
Rutherford, Ward, *The Druids and Their Heritage.* London: Gordon & Cremonesi, 1978.
Sandoz, Mari, *These Were the Sioux.* New York: Hastings, 1961.
Schlesinger, Arthur M., Jr., *The Coming of the New Deal.* Boston: Houghton Mifflin, 1958.
Schwartz, Stephan A.:
The Alexandria Project. New York: Delacorte Press, 1983.
"Psychic Search." *Omni,* April 1981.
The Secret Vaults of Time. New York: Grosset & Dunlap, 1978.
Severin, Tim:
"The Quest for Ulysses." *National Geographic,* August 1986.
The Ulysses Voyage: Sea Search for the Odyssey. New York: E. P. Dutton, 1987.
Sharkey, John, *Celtic Mysteries: The Ancient Religion.* New York: Crossroad, 1975.
Sillar, Frederick Cameron, and Ruth Mary Meyler, *Cats: Ancient & Modern.* London: Studio Vista, 1966.
"Solomon's Mines Found?" *Science News,* May 29, 1976.
Stiebing, William H., Jr.:
Ancient Astronauts, Cosmic Collisions. Buffalo, N.Y.: Prometheus Books, 1984.
"Futile Quest: The Search for Noah's Ark." *The Biblical Archaeology Review,* June 1976.
Stirling, Matthew W., "Discovering the New World's Oldest Dated Work of Man." *The National Geographic Magazine,* August 1939.
Storm, Hyemeyohsts, *Seven Arrows.* New York: Ballantine

Books, 1972.
Strange Stories, Amazing Facts. Pleasantville, N.Y.: Reader's Digest Association, 1977.
Sulzberger, Jean, ed., *Search.* New York: Harper & Row, 1979.
Thompson, Stith, *Motif-Index of Folk-Literature* (Vol. 1). Bloomington: Indiana University Press, 1955.
Thorndike, Joseph J., Jr., ed., *Discovery of Lost Worlds.* New York: American Heritage, 1979.
Tolstoy, Nikolai, *The Quest for Merlin.* Boston: Little, Brown, 1985.
Vawter, Bruce, *A Path through Genesis.* New York: Sheed & Ward, 1956.
"Wallace Letters." *Newsweek,* March 22, 1948.
Webster's New Biographical Dictionary. Springfield, Mass.: Merriam-Webster, 1988.
Westwood, Jennifer, ed., *The Atlas of Mysterious Places.* New York: Weidenfeld & Nicolson, 1987.
Wilcox, Robert K., *Shroud.* New York: Macmillan, 1977.
Wilson, David A., "The Search for the Holy Grail." *Fate,* March 1990.
Wilson, Ian:
The Turin Shroud. London: Victor Gollancz, 1978.
Undiscovered. London: Michael O'Mara Books, 1987.
Winstone, H. V. F., *Uncovering the Ancient World.* London: Constable, 1985.
Wood, Michael, *In Search of the Trojan War.* New York: Facts On File, 1985.
Wyatt, Ronald E., *Discovered: Noah's Ark!* Nashville: World Bible Society, 1989.

INDEX

Numerals in italics indicate an illustration of the subject mentioned.

A

B

C

S

T

U

V

W

Y

Z

TIME-LIFE BOOKS
EUROPEAN EDITOR: Ellen Phillips
Design Director: Ed Skyner
Director of Editorial Resources: Samantha Hill
Chief Sub-Editor: Ilse Gray

First European English language printing 1992.

ISBN 0 7054 0699 7

MYSTERIES OF THE UNKNOWN

SERIES EDITOR: Jim Hicks
Series Administrator: Jane A. Martin
Art Director: Ellen Robling
Picture Editor: Susan V. Kelly

Editorial Staff for *Mystic Quests*
Text Editors: Robert A. Doyle (principal), Janet Cave
Senior Writer: Esther R. Ferington
Associate Editors/Research: Christian D. Kinney, Gwen Mullen, Jacqueline L. Shaffer
Assistant Art Director: Susan M. Gibas
Writer: Sarah D. Ince
Senior Copy Coordinators: Colette Stockum
Copy Coordinators: Donna Carey, Juli Duncan
Picture Coordinators: Julia Kendrick, Michael Kentoff
Editorial Assistant: Donna Fountain

Special Contributors: Terrell Smith (lead research); Patty U. Chang, Ann Louise Gates, Mimi Harrison, Evelyn S. Pretty-man, Nancy J. Seeger (research); Sarah Brash, Margery A. duMond, Mark A. Fischetti, Donál Kevin Gordon, Lydia Preston Hicks, Harvey S. Loomis, Daniel Stashower (text); Sara Schneidman, William H. Stiebing, Jr. (consultants); John Drummond (design); Barbara L. Klein (index).

Correspondents: Elisabeth Kraemer-Singh (Bonn), Christine Hinze (London), Christina Lieberman (New York), Maria Vincenza Aloisi (Paris), Ann Natanson (Rome). Valuable assistance was also provided by Mehmet Ali Kislali, Serpil Gogen (Ankara); Elizabeth Brown, Barbara Gevene Hertz (Copenhagen); Judy Aspinall (London); Kathryn White (New York); Ann Wise, Leonora Dodsworth (Rome).

This volume is one of a series that examines the history and nature of seemingly paranormal phenomena.

Colour reproduction by Liberty Engraving Co., Chicago, U.S.A.
Printed and bound by R.R. Donnelley & Sons Co., Willard, Ohio, U.S.A.